DANCING TO THE HEARTBEAT OF GOD

Stories of discipleship

The Archbishop of Canterbury's
Lent Book 2026

The Anglican Communion

First published in Great Britain in 2026
SPCK Publishing
Part of the SPCK Group, Studio 101, The Record Hall,
16–16A Baldwin's Gardens, London EC1N 7RJ
spckpublishing.co.uk

Text copyright © SPCK 2026

The authors of the individual chapters included in this work have asserted their rights under the Copyright, Designs and Patents Act, 1988, to be identified as such.

All rights reserved. No part of this book may be reproduced or transmitted in any form or by any means, electronic or mechanical, including photocopying, recording, or by any information storage and retrieval system, without permission in writing from the publisher.

No part of this book may be used or reproduced in any manner for the purpose of training artificial intelligence technologies or systems.

SPCK does not necessarily endorse the individual views contained in its publications.

Scripture quotations marked CSB are taken from the Christian Standard Bible®, Anglicized Edition, Copyright © 2017 by Holman Bible Publishers. Used by permission. Christian Standard Bible® and CSB® are federally registered trademarks of Holman Bible Publishers.

Scripture quotations marked ESV are taken from the ESV Bible (The Holy Bible, English Standard Version), Anglicized Edition, copyright © 2001 by Crossway, a publishing ministry of Good News Publishers. Used by permission. All rights reserved.

Scripture quotations marked NIV are taken from The Holy Bible, New International Version (Anglicized edition). Copyright © 1979, 1984, 2011 by Biblica. Used by permission of Hodder & Stoughton Ltd, an Hachette UK company. All rights reserved. 'NIV' is a registered trademark of Biblica. UK trademark number 1448790.

Scripture quotations marked NKJV are taken from the New King James Version. Copyright © 1982 by Thomas Nelson, Inc. Used by permission. All rights reserved.

Scripture quotations marked NRSV are taken from the New Revised Standard Version of the Bible, Anglicized Edition, copyright © 1989, 1995 by the Division of Christian Education of the National Council of the Churches of Christ in the USA. Used by permission. All rights reserved.

EU GPSR Authorised Representative
LOGOS EUROPE, 9 rue Nicolas Poussin, 17000, La Rochelle, France
Email: Contact@logoseurope.eu

British Library Cataloguing-in-Publication Data
A catalogue record for this book is available from the British Library

ISBN 978-0-281-09231-4
eBook ISBN 978-0-281-09230-7

1 3 5 7 9 10 8 6 4 2

Typeset by Westchester Publishing Services
First printed in Great Britain by Clays Ltd

eBook by Westchester Publishing Services

Produced on paper from sustainable sources

Contents

Foreword by Sarah Mullally, Archbishop of Canterbury designate — ix

Introduction by Stephen Cottrell, Archbishop of York — 1

WEEK 1

The prophetic witness of friendship — 7
Justin Duckworth, Archbishop in the Province of Aotearoa New Zealand and Polynesia

Giving your faith for others — 12
Albert Chama, Archbishop of Central Africa and Bishop of Lusaka

Rebirth with the river: the simplicity of faith in the Amazon — 17
Marinez Rosa dos Santos Bassotto, Bishop of the Anglican diocese of Amazonia and Primate Bishop of the Anglican Episcopal Church of Brazil

Belonging together: discipleship across the Communion — 21
Maggie Swinson, Chair of the Anglican Consultative Council

Contents

WEEK 2

An interview conversation conducted by Bishop Riscylla Shaw　29
With Annie Ittoshat, Suffragan Bishop of the diocese of the Arctic

Waiting in hope　34
Mark Short, Primate of the Anglican Church of Australia

Why people still come to church: voices from Southern Africa　39
Thabo Makgoba, Archbishop of Cape Town and Metropolitan of the Anglican Church in Southern Africa

Following Christ in every season of life　46
Brian Williams, Anglican Bishop of Argentina and Presiding Bishop of the Anglican Church of South America

WEEK 3

A widow's might　53
Jo Bailey Wells, Deputy Secretary General and Bishop for Episcopal Ministry in the Anglican Communion

Walking with the least　58
David Eisho Uehara, Primate of Japan and Bishop of Okinawa (Anglican Church in Japan)

Contents

Renewing our baptismal covenant as a Lenten practice — 61
DeDe Duncan-Probe, Bishop of the Episcopal diocese of Central New York

Discipleship as relationships — 65
Sammy Wainaina, Adviser to the Archbishop of Canterbury on Anglican Communion Affairs

When there are no words to pray — 69
Shane Parker, Primate of All Canada

WEEK 4

Giving your faith for others — 75
Maimbo Mndolwa, Diocesan Bishop of Tanga (Tanzania)

'Not my will but yours be done' — 79
Anthony Ball, Director of the Anglican Centre in Rome

The expanse of the thin veil — 84
Helen Kennedy, Bishop of the diocese of Qu'Appelle (Canada)

'The kingdom of God is in your midst' — 89
Stephen Than Myint Oo, Archbishop of Myanmar and Bishop of Yangon

Contents

WEEK 5

A compelling community — 97
Anashuya Fletcher, Sri Lankan-born Assistant Bishop in the Anglican diocese of Wellington (New Zealand)

'My Lord and My God': confessing Christ amid trials — 101
B. K. Nayak, Moderator, Synod of the Church of North India (CNI)

'All you need is love' (The Beatles) — 106
Anne Germond, Bishop of the diocese of Algoma (Canada) and Metropolitan of the Ecclesiastical Province of Ontario

Discipleship stories from the Anglican Communion — 110
Anthony Poggo, Secretary General of the Anglican Communion

WEEK 6

Listening: a Lenten devotion — 119
Riscylla Shaw, Suffragan Bishop in the diocese of Toronto

Why people in Butere follow Christ — 125
Rose Okeno, Bishop of Butere (Kenya)

Contents

Looking at the world with new eyes   129
Graham Tomlin, former Bishop of Kensington,
editor-in-chief of SeenandUnseen.com

The reasons why people follow Christ in our context   133
David Alvarado, Primate of the Anglican
Church in Central America and Diocesan
Bishop of El Salvador

Discipleship stories from the Anglican Communion   138
Sean W. Rowe, Presiding Bishop and Primate
of The Episcopal Church

Afterword: Confidence in the gospel   142
Sarah Mullally, Archbishop of
Canterbury designate

Notes   147

Foreword

'Go into all the world and proclaim the gospel to the whole of creation.'
(Mark 16:15, NRSV)

It's hard to think of a more rousing verse in the Bible. It's perhaps also hard to think of one more daunting! It's not a small ask – it really couldn't be bigger – and so where do we even start? How should we go about it?

That's where this book comes in. Every year, the Archbishop of Canterbury's Lent Book is published to offer encouragement and inspiration to the Church of England. To guide us through the trials of Lent, and to build our confidence in proclaiming the gospel.

This year, it is slightly different – firstly, because we have not had an Archbishop of Canterbury in post since January, and won't until the Confirmation of my Election in January. I'm very grateful to Alison Barr, Publisher at SPCK, and Tosin Oladipo, Chaplain to the Archbishop of Canterbury, for guiding the creation of this book in this period of vacancy, and to Archbishop Stephen Cottrell, Mark Steadman, Everlyne Gitau, Bishop Anthony Poggo and the Anglican Communion Office for their invaluable help.

But there is another, more profound difference. Because those same figures had an inspired vision – that this iteration of the Lent Book would extend its horizon beyond the Church

Foreword

of England, and be written by and from the worldwide Anglican Communion.

And so this iteration is richer and more diverse than any of its predecessors, in that it comprises around thirty authors from across the globe, all sharing what it means to dance to the heartbeat of God in their own contexts. It encapsulates the wonderful diversity across our Communion, but also our unity, through our shared faith and witness.

My prayer is that the stories in each chapter of this book will serve as true inspiration and encouragement for you this Lent, and give us all the confidence to go into the world and proclaim the gospel to the whole of creation.

Sarah Mullally
Archbishop of Canterbury designate

Introduction

What a blessed relief that Cleopas and his companion weren't Anglicans – or at least not Church of England Anglicans. If they had been, then I fear that having encountered and recognised Jesus in the breaking of the bread, they would have called over the waiter, ordered a couple of large brandies, sat back in the leather armchairs in the snug of the inn at Emmaus and simply discussed the marvels they had experienced, but not actually done very much about it. They might even have suggested writing an academic paper on the subject.

But, no, this isn't what happened. There and then, that very moment, they rise up and rush back to Jerusalem. They couldn't wait to share with others the good news they had experienced and received.

This, surely, is the authenticating mark of discipleship. Our encounter with the risen Lord – whether it be sudden and astonishing, like the breaking of bread at Emmaus, or slow and full of questions and discussion, like the walk to Emmaus itself – is good news for ourselves, but also good news for everyone. Indeed, it's good news to be shared with the whole world.

This is why in the Gospels there isn't a moment when the twelve people we call the disciples graduate to become the same twelve people we call the apostles. They are always both. They are always those who are constantly learning from Jesus and those who are consistently sent out by Jesus; those who are gathered together as followers, and those who are on apostolic mission. So, in the Church of England when we speak about being a Jesus-shaped Church, we use the language of missionary discipleship, seeking to be those who learn from our encounter with Jesus to become those who share what they have received with others. We want to be renewed in our faith and our witness by becoming the apostolic Church.

Lent is a time of preparation for Easter. It is like a walk to Emmaus where we talk with Jesus, open the Scriptures and learn more about what our faith means – for us and for the world. It leads to the great celebration of the paschal mystery, where we reaffirm our baptismal promises and commit ourselves afresh to be the Church that Jesus sends out today.

* * *

In this book you will find stories of experience and encounter; of prayer, discipleship, learning and mission from all around the Anglican Communion. What each story has in common is that it begins with an encounter with Jesus and then discovers that one of the best ways of sustaining that encounter and building that relationship with Jesus is to rise up and share it.

The astonishing account of missionary discipleship that we find in chapter 24 of Luke's Gospel has one last little twist in the tale. We don't usually spot it, since when we read the passage in church we tend to finish at verse 35, with the disciples rushing back to Jerusalem and telling their story. However, if you read on, you discover that, as they recount what has happened, Jesus comes and stands among them again (Luke 24:36).

Introduction

This is another of the authenticating marks of discipleship. We are inspired, resourced and enabled by our encounter with Jesus; we instinctively know that it is given to be shared, but Jesus is not our possession, not a mascot round our neck. As the Holy Spirit sends us out on mission, so Jesus is revealed afresh, present in those to whom we are sent, often waiting to be named and made known, but always standing among us, and always there before us.

I'm not quite sure I experience this every day, but hardly a week goes by when God does not open a door for me both to share the love of Christ *with* others and to find that love *in* others. And, just as on the Emmaus Road Jesus' first words are a question (Luke 24:17), often it is the refining fire of the questions of those who are not yet Christians which deepen our understanding (Luke 24:17).

As you read *Dancing to the Heartbeat of God*, receive these stories and prepare for Easter, I hope that your heart will burn within you as was the case for Cleopas and his companion on the first Easter Day. And that Jesus will be revealed to you afresh.

Stephen Cottrell
Archbishop of York

WEEK 1

The prophetic witness of friendship

The Most Revd Justin Duckworth became Archbishop in the Province of Aotearoa New Zealand and Polynesia in May 2024. Since 1992, this province has had a shared leadership model in which each of the three *tikanga* (ethnic expressions) have their own archbishop and share governance of the Church. Justin is Archbishop of Tikanga Pākehā, those who make their home in Aotearoa New Zealand through the signing of its foundational document, the Treaty of Waitangi (1840). He has also held the role of Bishop of the diocese of Wellington since 2010. His background is in youth and pioneer ministry – he cofounded the modern monastic order Urban Vision which seeks to provide a Jesus presence to those who find themselves at the margins of their communities.

> As a prisoner for the Lord, then, I urge you to live a life worthy of the calling you have received. Be completely humble and gentle; be patient, bearing with one another in love. Make every effort to keep the unity of the Spirit through the bond of peace. There is one body and one Spirit, just as you were called to one hope when you were called; one Lord, one faith, one baptism; one God

Week 1

and Father of all, who is over all and through all and in all.
(Ephesians 4:1–6, NIV)

Although it's more usual for bishops to live where their cathedral is based, in 2018 my wife Jenny and I moved to the north of the diocese of Wellington. We had felt the call to strengthen the Anglican communities of faith there, and to help plant a new Urban Vision residential expression.

We eventually found ourselves in one of the outlying suburbs of the city of Whanganui. Exhibiting all the markers of high social deprivation, the area often feels like a forgotten community. With a small team, we based ourselves at a parish which had lain fallow for many years and began to pray and explore what God was up to there. We weren't the only ones who had felt called to this place. Several years earlier, a Pentecostal church plant had responded to God's invitation to make a home in this same neighbourhood.

In time, I found myself becoming good mates with the Pentecostal pastor. On days off, we'll hang out. Our families have meals together. I dragged him around his first marathon. Our church families do life collectively too – sharing big events like Easter and community Christmas carols.

Nonetheless, we'd both agree that we sit at polar opposites on most of the hot topics that take up church airtime. For example, he is a Trump supporter and would describe himself as Zionist. The Israeli flag hangs in his church. In contrast, I marched the distance of the Gaza Strip in support of ending Israeli occupation of the Occupied Palestinian Territory.

Hospitality beyond ideology

In 2019, New Zealand began its COVID-19 lockdowns, and the government mandated that vaccines be administered to all citizens. Our country's approach was initially widely lauded, but in time, the ongoing toll of isolation resulted in large-scale protest, including the longest occupation of Parliament grounds by those who were anti-mandate or anti-vaccination.

While I was photographed happily receiving my vaccination through the car window, my pastor friend and his church were definitely on the vaccine-hesitant end of the spectrum. Their church lawn hosted the kind of protest placards that made those of a more moderate viewpoint turn their heads.

Local government health officials had set up a vaccine centre in our neighbourhood at the only place they could find – on the road beside the local café. Worried that this was unsafe for those who were coming to receive their injections, my friend invited the officials to move the station to his church lawn next door. Here, plain to see, was the anti-vax leader welcoming those he disagreed with in order to show that the hospitality of Christ was more important to him than acting in accordance with his personal views. It was an amazing witness to the love of Jesus.

'Every effort' as prophetic witness

As I live into this relationship, I continue to appreciate the generosity and love I see in my friend.

We still disagree, but we make sure that we have real conversations and usually find our disagreement is not as big as we thought it was. This is because we are careful not to fall into the trap of 'othering'. Paul writes in the letter to the Ephesians of the need to 'make *every effort*' to seek unity in the Spirit. In practice, for me and my friend, that means choosing deliberately to go across the divide and appreciate that there may be treasure on the other side. Hospitality helps, as Jesus knew, having sat around many tables. So too does refusing to break the world into 'goodies and baddies'.

Seeking unity remains critically important in our global context, not just within the Church but as we bear witness to a world which tries to divide. The Church at its best is one of the few places where people – in their beautiful difference – come together, gathering around the table of the King.

The great work of the gospel is reconciliation. On the cross, Jesus opened his arms to both of the men being crucified alongside him. Ultimately, one prisoner chose a relationship of life and the other didn't, yet it was still Jesus stretched out between them. Often, in the midst of differences within our church context, we fail to remember that both sides have chosen to follow Jesus. When we forget this, our witness to the world suffers.

Micro-stories

The story of my friend and me is not grand or impressive; it's just a tale of two people intentionally seeking to be in relationship despite the things we disagree on. But although the story is not grand or impressive, it does reveal the power that's available to each one of us when we step into relationship. My prayer is that all who follow Jesus will have stories of friendship to tell, in which we are able to say that what unites us is greater than what divides us. In relating those stories, we provide a prophetic witness to a polarised world of the reconciling work Christ accomplished for all on the cross.

Prayer

Lord God, your heart so desired the reconciliation of all people that you sent your only Son to achieve what we could not. We praise you for this gift and ask that you help us to live lives worthy of the calling we have received through the cross. As your people, may we be empowered by your Spirit to have simple stories of deep friendship across division to share, so that the world may know that the relationship Jesus offers is open to all. Amen.

Questions for reflection

1 *He aha te mea nui te ao? He tangata he tangata, he tangata* ('What is the most important thing in the world? It is people, it is people, it is people'). This Māori proverb places ultimate importance on relationships. How do you see this reflected in the life of Jesus?
2 Have you ever had to compromise on an issue you felt strongly about in order to reconcile or prioritise a relationship? What happened?
3 Can you think of a relationship that you have with someone who is very different from you? What tangible action could you take this Lent to strengthen that relationship?

Giving your faith for others

The Most Revd Albert Chama was born in the mining town of Kitwe on the Copperbelt in Zambia, the third in a family of nine boys and a girl. After school, he worked in various industries before responding to God's call to the religious life, as a Franciscan friar in Zimbabwe. He later attended Bishop Gaul College in Harare and the University of Zimbabwe, before moving to the UK for postgraduate studies at the University of Birmingham, where he obtained a master's degree in Community Development. In 2003, Albert was consecrated Bishop for the Anglican diocese of Northern Zambia. Twenty-one years later, he became Archbishop of the Province of Central Africa, and he currently serves as Metropolitan Bishop of the Anglican diocese of Lusaka, after being translated from the diocese of Northern Zambia.

Discipleship in Zambia: a path of faith, service and transformation

In the heart of Zambia, a country with a rich Christian heritage, discipleship is not only a theological term: it's a lived experience. Picture, if you will, a small village on the outskirts of Lusaka, where a group of men, women and children gather in a humble church building made from locally sourced materials – mud bricks, thatched roofs and wooden beams. As the sun sets over the African horizon, the church becomes a sanctuary for the local community, a space where discipleship is not only taught but woven into the fabric of daily existence. Here, taking on an intimate and tangible form, it is evident in the farmer who, despite his struggles with unpredictable weather, still tithes a portion of his harvest. It may be seen in the young mother with a child on her back, who listens attentively to the word of God and teaches her children to pray before meals. It is demonstrated by the elder who visits the sick in the local clinic, offering prayer, comfort and companionship.

A personal journey: discipleship through the eyes of a Zambian bishop

When I reflect on my ministry as a bishop in Zambia, and the way I have come to understand discipleship, my thoughts turn to a man of deep humility and unwavering faith who has been a beacon for many in his diocese. This church leader's approach to ministry embodies the very essence of what it means to be a disciple of Christ – not only to follow, but to lead others into a transformative relationship with Jesus. Rooted in a profound understanding of the gospel and embedded in the local culture and the daily lives of his people, he regards discipleship as a call to action. It's about walking alongside others in their everyday struggles, joys and aspirations; it's about sharing theological knowledge *and* offering emotional, spiritual and practical support.

Week 1

I often recall a particular incident involving this church leader which took place when he visited a rural village on a rainy Sunday morning. Despite the downpour flooding the dirt roads and making travel almost impossible, many of the congregants valiantly showed up to worship. The church leader, similarly undeterred by the weather, had arrived hours early, and as people trickled in, he moved through the crowd, greeting individuals by name, praying with the elderly, laughing with the children and listening to the concerns of the young couples. Informal and kind, his pastoral care nurtured genuine relationship.

During lunch after the service, the leader invited local farmers to share their struggles. One by one, they spoke about the challenges they faced due to crop failure, rising costs and the difficulty of providing for their families. In response, they were offered words of encouragement, listened to with empathy, prayed for individually and, in several instances, connected with community resources and agricultural experts who could help. This was discipleship in action – a leader walking alongside his people, showing them the love of Christ not only through words, but through tangible acts of care.

What stood out most was his attitude towards mentoring young people. Rooted in trust and intentional investment, his concern was not simply to preach to them but to take time to walk with them, encourage their talents and hold them accountable in their spiritual growth.

The result of this approach is that many of the young leaders in the church have grown into passionate servants of Christ, actively engaging in outreach programmes, youth ministries and community development projects. The church's investment in the younger generation shows commitment to a discipleship model that goes beyond personal faith into the realm of communal responsibility.

The challenge of discipleship in Zambia today

In a broader context Zambia, like many other African nations, faces a range of social, economic and political issues that affect its people's ability to live out their faith in practical ways. Poverty, unemployment, inadequate healthcare, the impact of HIV/AIDS, gender injustice and, in recent times, the impact of climate change, have left many communities struggling.

In these circumstances, discipleship takes on an even more profound meaning. It calls for more than a Sunday morning faith. It calls for disciples who are willing to stand with the vulnerable, to bring hope to the hopeless and to make sacrifices for the sake of others.

Conclusion: discipleship as a lifelong journey

Discipleship in Zambia, then, is a lived reality that reflects the struggles and joys of the people. The ministry of a bishop embodies what it means to be a disciple in the context of this beautiful, complex country. It is to be on a continuous journey – one that involves walking with others, sharing in their burden and lifting them up to experience the transformative power of Christ.

Week 1

As the sun sets over the Zambian landscape and the village church becomes a place of refuge once more, the call to discipleship remains ever-present. It is both a challenge and a privilege; one that invites each believer to become an agent of change in their world.

Rebirth with the river: the simplicity of faith in the Amazon

The Most Revd Marinez Rosa dos Santos Bassotto is Diocesan Bishop of the Anglican diocese of Amazonia and Primate Bishop of the Anglican Episcopal Church of Brazil. She resides in Belém do Pará in the Amazon, where her ministry is intertwined with a deep commitment to defending the environment and the rights of indigenous and traditional populations; dedicating herself to the care of God's creation and socio-environmental justice; and seeing creation as the first revelation of God.

The Amazon, with its vast and rich biodiversity, is the location of my ministry and my journey of discipleship. Here, where rivers are our roads and the forest is our home, the vibrant presence of life is a constant reminder of the rhythm of God's heart.

It was during one of my regular walks that I met Mr Antônio Dias on the banks of the Tocantins River. An elderly riverside dweller, he had lived his entire life in the Cametá region of Pará. He told me about his struggle to protect his community and his dream of restoring the area's long-lost biodiversity. He spoke of how, when he was a child, everything worked in harmony: there was the flooding and drying of the river; there was the right time to fish for each species of fish and the right time to harvest each type of fruit that the forest offered. But now, everything had changed.

'Bishop, in the old days, the river rose and fell, and we learned to live with it. Each flood was a new beginning.'

This image of the river, which floods and recedes, purifies and fertilises, offers us a profound parable for the season of Lent. Lent is not just a liturgical season; it is an invitation to the gestation of a new being.

* * *

Lent invites us to accompany Jesus on his journey into the desert. The desert evokes images of sand and solitude. Here in the Amazon, however, we are conscious that the desert can take many forms. We bear responsibility ourselves for some painful creations, such as the deserts of misery that ravage entire communities; the violence of wars that devastate bodies and souls; the intolerance that divides us, and the deforestation that transforms forests into arid lands. There are also the deserts of arrogance that prevent us from listening to ancestral wisdom; of greed that exploit without limits; of selfishness that isolate us, and of apathy and condescension that prevent us from acting.

As bishop in this region, I witness the struggle against these deserts on a daily basis. I see the resilience of the Indigenous riverine and traditional peoples who, despite centuries of marginalisation and constant threats to their land and way of life, continue to defend the forest, knowing that their lives are intrinsically linked to it.

Rebirth with the river: the simplicity of faith in the Amazon

* * *

The season of Lent also invites us to be 'born again' (John 3:3, NIV). This feels somewhat radical. How can we be born again, especially as adults, burdened as we are with experiences, certainties and, at times, the weariness that life imposes?

In the Amazon, rebirth is a daily necessity – not only spiritually, but in terms of how we choose to inhabit this planet. We are born again when we recognise that creation is not a resource to be exploited, but a sacred gift to be cherished. We are born again when we shed the anthropocentric view that places us above all things, and embrace an integral ecology where everything is interconnected. Our commitment to defending the environment and the rights of Indigenous peoples is the living expression of discipleship in this context. In short, we need to be born into a new way of relating to creation and to our neighbours in order to see the kingdom of God.

During Lent, we are reminded of Jesus' words in Mark 10:15 about receiving the kingdom of God like a child. This will involve abandoning our intellectual complications, our hesitations and the weight of 'adult wisdom' that often distances us from God and his creation. Instead, we are called to trust with the simplicity and hope of children, even when the path is arduous and painful; even when it passes through the cross.

* * *

To be a disciple in the Amazon is to follow Jesus in his radical commitment to life. It is to fight so that rivers are not dammed, forests are not burned and cultures are not silenced.

It is to embrace the pain of creation groaning (Romans 8:22) and work so that it can breathe and flourish again. It is to have faith that God wants to flood our lives with joy and our families with blessings, and grant us eternal life which begins now, in the loving care of what he has entrusted to us.

This Lent, may the river of God wash away the deserts of our hearts and our world. May we be reborn, like the waters of the Amazon, with a simple and deep faith, ready to follow Jesus.

Prayer

God of all creation, in this season of Lent, purify our hearts and minds. Help us to be born again, to strip ourselves of arrogance and greed, and to embrace the simplicity and trust of children. May we see your kingdom in every leaf, in every river, in every face of your sons and daughters. Give us the courage and faithfulness to follow in Jesus' footsteps, defending life in all its forms. Amen.

Questions for reflection

1 How can you contribute to protecting God's creation in your community?
2 What areas of your life need a 'new birth' in the light of Lent?
3 What does it mean for you to receive the kingdom of God with the simplicity and trust of a child?

Belonging together: discipleship across the Communion

Maggie Swinson serves as Chair of the Anglican Consultative Council, having previously been its Vice Chair and the Church of England's lay representative. Her work as Company Secretary at Primary Care 24 in Liverpool has given her wide governance experience which she brings to her roles as Chair of the Liverpool Diocesan Schools Trust and the Diocesan Board of Finance. Maggie is committed to building fellowship across the Anglican Communion through listening, mutual respect and shared faith.

For many years, the Anglican Communion was something I knew about in theory rather than something I experienced as a reality. It appeared in church reports and mission statements but didn't touch my daily life. That changed in 1991, when I attended the World Council of Churches Assembly. I went there committed to ecumenism and came home with a new understanding of what it means to be an Anglican and a deeper love for our tradition.

As part of the meeting there were sessions called 'Family Meetings', where representatives from each confessional family – Anglicans, Lutherans and others – gathered together. For the first time, I found myself in a room filled with

Anglicans from across the world. In meeting them and hearing their stories, the Communion became real for me – not as an organisation, but as a fellowship of people who shared the same faith and hope and the familiar rhythm of prayer and sacrament. Although I enjoyed much of the worship, it was in the Anglican services that I felt at home – a quiet reminder that our liturgy is one of the threads that binds us across the world.

I had been a member of the Church of England's General Synod since 1985 but after that experience I was more attuned to reports from the Anglican Consultative Council (ACC). On one occasion, while we were listening to such a report, the person sitting next to me said, 'I think that one day you will be our lay representative on the ACC.' At the time, it seemed unlikely – but in 2012 he was proved right and I attended my first ACC meeting, in Auckland, as the lay representative for the Church of England.

That occasion remains a vivid memory. In those days, the gatherings lasted for two weeks, combining business with opportunities to engage locally. Spouses were invited, and my husband Michael joined me. The Church in Aotearoa New Zealand and Polynesia is structured in three Tikangas – Māori, Pākehā and Pacifica – and each hosted an evening for the Council. We feasted royally with the Māori, enjoyed fine dining with the Pākehā, and shared a deeply moving time with the Pacifica.

That third evening combined wonderful hospitality with a presentation about the effects of climate change on the Pacific islands – something that has never left Michael and me. As we were departing, one of those present spoke to us, pleading that we take the climate issues seriously and that we encourage others to do the same. He said quietly, 'Help us; we are desperate.' In that moment, the Communion became even more real – a family whose members' lives and hopes are bound together, across oceans and circumstances. Their suffering was no distant theory, but ours to share.

Since then, I have seen that truth again and again. The ACC gathers people from across the Communion to listen to one another, to discern God's call and to serve together. It is not a parliament, but a fellowship of mutual learning and shared discipleship. I first joined the ACC as a member, later served as Vice Chair, and was elected Chair at our meeting in Accra in 2023. These roles have never felt like offices to hold, but opportunities to pay heed to the Spirit.

Yet, I have always been aware that many in the Church of England do not feel that sense of belonging to the wider Communion. The Communion can seem distant, something 'out there', rather than a fellowship we are part of every day. I hope that by sharing these stories, others might feel more connected to this global family.

Some years ago, in 2015, a member of staff at the Anglican Communion Office posted a message on social media that touched me profoundly: 'If you have friends in Burundi, pray for peace. If you are a member of the body of Christ, you have friends in Burundi.' I have shared those words many times since, because they express so perfectly what it means to belong. Our fellowship is not a concept or a committee – it is relationship. When one part rejoices, we all rejoice; when one part suffers, we all pray and care.

Week 1

That belonging has deepened for me through visits to many parts of the Communion. In Sudan, I called on a church that turned its courtyard into an open classroom after school – chalkboards lining the walls – so that local children could come for extra lessons. In a country where Christians are a small minority, the Church's quiet service spoke volumes. In Alexandria, Egypt, I saw discipleship lived out through the provision of education and healthcare – early years teaching in some of the most deprived areas, linked with the monitoring and treatment of anaemia and worms, so that children could learn well. In Mozambique and Angola, a new province was born, giving people the joy of worshipping and reading Scripture in their local language, and doing their work in the nations' official language of Portuguese rather than in the English they had had to use when they were part of the province of Southern Africa. In Chile, I met lay people whose energy for discipleship and leadership was contagious, and among the Mapuche in the mountains, faith was intertwined with creation itself: a reminder that God's grace is as wide as the earth.

Through these encounters, I have learned that discipleship itself is not theory but a lived reality. Across the Communion, people follow Christ in ways shaped by their culture and context – but always marked by the same hope.

My service as Chair has also taken me beyond Anglican circles. I attended the Primates' Meeting in Rome, where we were received by Pope Francis. Later, I was honoured to represent the Communion at his funeral, and again at the inaugural Mass of Pope Leo. Standing in St Peter's, surrounded by Christians from every tradition, I was reminded that our belonging stretches far beyond the Anglican family, into the whole body of Christ.

And yet, whenever I need reminding of what unity really looks like, I think of one particular moment, when – as the ACC, its Standing Committee, the Primates' Meeting or the Lambeth Conference – we pray the Lord's Prayer together, each in the language that comes most naturally to us. There is a beauty and resonance to the sound and a unity unlike anything I experience elsewhere.

This Lent, as we walk again in the way of the cross, perhaps we might pause at those first words: '*Our* Father'. Not *my* Father, but *our* Father. To belong to Christ is to belong to one another – across borders, languages and cultures. And in that belonging, we discover again the joy and the challenge of following him.

Prayer

Gracious God,
you call us to belong not only to you
but to one another in the body of Christ.
Teach us to rejoice with those who rejoice,
and to share the burdens of those who
      suffer.
Draw us closer to the life of your
      worldwide Church
and make us signs of your grace in the
      world.
Amen.

Questions for reflection
1 I write that I discovered the Anglican Communion as a family rather than an organisation. When have you felt most aware of belonging to the wider Church – beyond your own parish?
2 If we really believe we are part of one worldwide body, how might that shape the way we pray for, give to or care for others in different places and situations?
3 Discipleship is something we live out together in every aspect of our lives. What helps you to see your faith as part of a shared journey with Christians around the world?

WEEK 2

An interview conversation conducted by Bishop Riscylla Shaw

The Rt Revd Annie Ittoshat is an Inuk Canadian bishop suffragan of the Anglican diocese of the Arctic. She is the first female Inuk bishop in the world. Raised in Kuujjuarapik, a community on Hudson Bay in Québec, Annie was ordained to the deaconate in 2006 and to the episcopate in 2019. She is married and mother to five children and has eight grandchildren. Annie is passionate about how faith and Inuit traditions guide our care for creation.

In the early 1980s, when I was 12 or 13 years old, the Pentecostal movement spread up north to my hometown, Kuujjuarapik. People were spending all night worshipping Jesus, praying by raising their arms in the air. It was winter, bitterly cold, and one evening, when the blizzard was so thick you couldn't see your hands in front of your face, I went with a friend to join her mom at a Pentecostal house-church meeting. That day, I received Jesus into my life. As I left, I was aware of a difference; a lightness that made me feel as if I could hop and jump.

Shortly afterwards, I met a boy I liked, and we got into partying. I went back to the ways of the world because I was just a kid and didn't know any better, and I stayed in that lifestyle

Week 2

for a long spell. Each time I got pregnant, I would stop smoking and drinking and try to get healthy again, but things were chaotic and scary, and I didn't feel safe.

At 29, pregnant with my third daughter, I began to think there had to be a better life.

* * *

I went to see an elderly Christian and told her that, when I was a kid, I had made a faith commitment. I said I didn't want to feel ashamed about that any more. She prayed a beautiful prayer for me, and right then, I sensed a shift, a change inside, as I recommitted my life to Christ.

Feeling secure and at peace and as if I'd been offered the chance to go in new direction, I wondered about returning to education. In due course, I enrolled at a college in Montréal and studied to become a social worker. That first semester, my cousin and I would meet up for a weekly Bible study. We could see that God was providing for us, directing our footsteps. I told my husband that I had given my life to Christ, and though as an Anglican he couldn't accept the Pentecostal style of worship, he respected the commitment I'd made and understood that I now wanted to go to church.

Just before we broke up for the Christmas holidays, I had a dream that a flood was going to hit my home community. I woke with butterflies in my stomach and phoned a Christian friend in Kuujjuaq.

When I told her about my dream, her response was, 'Let's pray.' Then the conversation turned to a different subject entirely as she said, 'This word keeps coming to me,

An interview conversation conducted by Bishop Riscylla Shaw

"Pangnirtung" and "the three-year ministry training programme".' That year's programme was supposed to have started but had been postponed.

In my heart, I knew that they were waiting for me! I said to God, 'Yes'.

After many years of training and carrying out ministry between Pangnirtung (a hamlet in Baffin Island) and Montréal, I now live and serve in Salluit, where I am also the priest-in-charge. As a bishop, I oversee 15 parish communities in northern Québec, for which we have four full-time priests, two deacons and many lay leaders for the places that don't have clergy. We count on these lay leaders as our frontline workers, even though they have full-time jobs being teachers, working for the town council and so on, and full plates dealing with whatever comes their way in family life.

There are no roads connecting the communities, so I get to them all by plane. I will often go visiting for four or five days at a time, depending on the weather (in winter, I'm sometimes stuck for longer). In Puvirnituq, for example, I'll stay with the priest; in other communities, with friends, family, my daughters or cousins.

Being called as a bishop is very different to being called as a priest. Even with the assurance that God will never leave us nor forsake us, bishops can sometimes feel lonely. I have had to dig deep many times. Sometimes, all I could do was pray and pray and pray. I've often asked, 'Lord, pour your love on these people. You won the victory, Lord, you are the life. Everything that we are dealing with is under your feet.'

Week 2

The reality is that there are always spiritual forces to contend with. We all make mistakes. I have to be humble enough to ask Jesus for forgiveness, so that my heart won't get hard. When something's gone wrong, I take a minute to think about my failings, share honestly with God, and then find a way to kneel down and pray.

* * *

About two or three years ago, I visited a small community that's under my oversight in Nunavut. We use four-wheelers to go visiting, so when I arrived, I went to the lay leader's house to borrow his. At church the next day, he told me that his wife was in the clinic, as she was really sick. After the service, we went around the homes of the elderly people who were not able to get out but wanted to have Holy Communion.

When we reached the lay leader's wife, she was responsive but couldn't sit up. Their grandkids were crying because they could see how sick she was. We prayed together, saying the Lord's Prayer, and shared Communion.

The next day, as I was getting ready to leave the community, I returned the four-wheeler to the lay leader and went to see his wife to say goodbye. Now she was sitting up.

'You were here, right, yesterday?'

'Yes, I was here. We had Communion, we prayed for you, and then we left. So, yes, I was here.'

'I remember you speaking. It was your voice, but you were wearing the doctor's coat.'

She told me that, in her spirit, she had gone up and been told, 'Your home is not quite ready, so you're going to go back.'

An interview conversation conducted by Bishop Riscylla Shaw

As priests, we often see our actions as regular day-to-day things: we say the Lord's Prayer, we share Communion, we pray for the sick. But in the midst of our ministry, Christ is alive.

That lady's story really opened my eyes. It is Christ who reaches out. It is Christ, risen from the dead, who is active in our lives. He healed that lady because her house was not quite ready.

We are the hands; he does the work.

Questions for reflection
1 Have you ever found yourself struggling and thinking that there has to be a better life?
2 What do you need to say to Jesus to help you to be honest with yourself and with God?
3 How can you be the hands of Christ in your community?

Waiting in hope

The Rt Revd Dr Mark Short took office as Primate of the Anglican Church of Australia in November 2025. He is married to Monica and previously served as Bishop of Canberra and Goulburn, a diverse urban and rural diocese centred on the nation's capital. Mark counts among his foundational discipleship experiences the gentle encouragement of a 75-year-old parishioner who walked alongside him in his teenage years, as well as the challenge of bearing witness to Jesus during his time as a journalist, and the joy of learning from South Sudanese and First Nations Christians.

The poet Emily Dickinson describes hope as a precious yet precarious bird that lives within the human soul (I paraphrase). Imagining hope in this way speaks to its value, but also to the need to nurture and protect it at a time when we can so easily give way to fear and cynicism.

Discipleship in my context

'We live in uncertain times' has been a political and cultural catchphrase in Australia over the past 12 months. Conflict at the international level and debates over identity and belonging at the national level contribute to uncertainty. For believers in

Jesus this is an opportunity to model and share the gracious confidence that comes from being grounded in the gospel. Local churches are engaging their communities through hospitality and service, for example by sponsoring and welcoming refugees and asylum seekers.

Between Easter and Pentecost 2025, all twenty-three Australian Anglican dioceses participated in a season of intentional outreach under the label Hope25. The hope that Jesus offers in uncertain times was shared through meals, art exhibitions, stalls, evangelistic courses and many other initiatives. One parish described the impact of Hope25 as follows:

> A deepening of faith and understanding of the hope we have in Jesus both individually and within our church family. A new boldness in sharing with people. The sense that our prayers and the prayers prayed right across Australia really did lead to open doors, open ears and soft hearts.

This uplifting testimony is related by Jacinta Moores:

> Two years ago, I was coming apart. I was going through a particularly hard time; I was exhausted – and I couldn't see much meaning in the shape my life had taken. But one day, underneath the pain, something strange happened. This wasn't just a thought or an idea – I suddenly felt a deep sense of knowing. I had this intense, quiet conviction that church would become a big part of my life. I had never been involved in any religion before, so this was pretty out of left field.

Week 2

I waited a whole year. Then one day, almost exactly twelve months later, a mum from my daughter's school casually asked if I wanted to come to church with her and her son. I didn't hesitate. I finally had my when and my where. I walked in the door that first Sunday and was completely overwhelmed with joy. I couldn't stop smiling. It was like a part of me that had been asleep my whole life suddenly woke up. I didn't understand everything that was happening, but I didn't need to. I just knew I was where I was meant to be.

I've been a single mum since I was a teenager. Life hasn't been gentle. I've had to be strong even when I felt completely alone. But this church community gave me something I've never had before – somewhere safe to land for me and for my daughter.

I was baptised in Lake Ginninderra on Easter Sunday 2025. The sky was clear, the water was warm, which is crazy for Canberra in autumn. My daughter was there, my family was there, and my church community showed up for me in a way I'll never forget. As I stood in that water, I felt everything – grief and joy; it was like coming home. It was incredibly powerful and real.

Hope, for me, isn't wishful thinking. It's the decision to believe that God is doing something even when I can't see it. Even when I don't have the foresight to know a year in advance that something is coming to me. It means I don't have to carry everything any more. I can stop gripping the wheel so tightly. I can 'let go and let God' – I used to say that before I even understood what it meant. Now I live it.

Reflection

For in this hope we were saved. But hope that is seen is no hope at all. Who hopes for what they already have? But if we hope for what we do not yet have, we wait for it patiently.
(Romans 8:24–25, NIV)

In Romans 8, Paul reminds believers that our present sufferings are the birth-pangs of the new creation built on the death and resurrection of the Lord Jesus Christ. Hope is not resignation – it is the Spirit-fuelled anticipation of a future more glorious than anything we might imagine.

Prayer
God of Hope
you call on us to be your witnesses in this
      uncertain world;
by your Spirit awaken in us
a true vision of your kingdom,
a greater certainty of our salvation, and
a deeper dedication to your service;
that through our words and actions the
      same Spirit may bring many who
      are lost to be found, and for them
      to celebrate the hope
that we can only have in Jesus Christ,
in whose name we pray. Amen.
(The Hope25 Collect)

Week 2

Questions for reflection
1 'Hope, for me, isn't wishful thinking. It's the decision to believe that God is doing something even when I can't see it.' How have you experienced this in your own life?
2 Read Romans 8:18–27. Recall a time when the Spirit has helped you in a time of weakness or suffering.

Why people still come to church: voices from Southern Africa

The Most Revd Dr Thabo Makgoba is the Archbishop of Cape Town and Metropolitan of the Anglican Church in Southern Africa. He was awarded the Cross of St Augustine by Archbishop Rowan Williams for his service to the Anglican Communion, and is currently one of the longest serving Primates within the Communion.

I write these reflections from Southern Africa, within the Anglican Church of this Province. The contexts here are in many ways different from that in the UK, but the questions are strikingly similar. Across Namibia, St Helena, Lesotho, Eswatini, South Africa and formerly Angola and Mozambique, I have reached out to bishops, clergy, retired leaders and lay members of the church, and to a Roman Catholic colleague, with a simple but searching question: why do people still attend church here?

I also gathered with young people at a youth Indaba in Taung, where fifty voices spoke candidly about their hopes and frustrations. Their concerns were sobering: inconsistent support from clergy, traditions that at times stifle creativity, and resistance to youthful vibrancy. Yet alongside these

Week 2

challenges, what emerged most strongly was a resilient joy and a deep attachment to the church as being at the heart of their lives.

What follows is not a survey but a collection of testimonies — stories, reflections and lived experiences. My prayer is that they might encourage you in the Church of England as you walk through this Lenten season: not as ready-made answers to complex challenges, but as a reminder that God's Spirit is still at work renewing the church wherever people gather with open hearts.

For many here, the reason for churchgoing is as simple and as profound as the Eucharist itself. To step into church is to encounter God in Word and Sacrament, to be fed with the bread of life, to remember that we are dependent on grace. The Eucharist binds us together across differences of age, class and background. It restores what is broken and re-centres life around Christ. Worship is not merely ritual but a lifeline.

We Southern Africans are a people of community who value a sense of belonging and identity. For us, the Church is not primarily an institution or a set of programmes. It is, quite literally, a family. Attendance is bound up with belonging, with being known and welcomed, and with carrying one another's burdens. The words of Archbishop Desmond Tutu resonate deeply: 'A person is a person through other persons.' This *ubuntu* — this conviction that our humanity is realised in relationship — is embodied in the church. To attend is to belong, to be woven into a fabric of love and care that sustains through hardship.

Worship also meets the individual needs of parishioners. One explained:

Church remains my safe space — the place that allows me to be in communion with Christ without the noise of the world intruding. It restores me after the week, and nourishes and anchors me for the days ahead. Without it, life is out of focus, like trying to read without glasses.

For others, church is a place of thanksgiving. 'I go to church to worship and give thanks to God for what he is doing in my life,' said one member. Another shared, 'Sunday is when I reunite with my spiritual family. It restores me, rebuilds me and rejuvenates me after the struggles of the week.'

For many parents, worship is also about witness to their children: 'I want to show and teach my children that there is always room for God, no matter what they take on in life,' says one. This language of family is significant.

A young Christian elaborated very simply on the point about joining a spiritual family: 'When I come to church, I reunite with my spiritual family just as surely as I return home to my family at the end of the day.'

In many communities, this belonging is expressed tangibly: congregations rally around bereaved families with both prayer and financial support; guilds and choirs wear uniforms that signal shared identity; indigenous languages and traditional clothing are woven into liturgy. Even practices such as *ukuxhoma ibhatyi* — hanging up a departed member's jacket — express how the church holds memory tenderly, ensuring that no one is forgotten.

Worship itself carries unique power. Structured liturgy, varied readings from Scripture, beloved hymns and the use of incense are all cherished. These are not seen as empty traditions but as rhythms that safeguard Christ at the centre. One informant noted, 'Our services are Christocentric; they do not leave room for distractions or strange theologies.' The breadth of readings – Old Testament, Psalm, Epistle, Gospel – provides a balanced engagement with Scripture. Hymns are loved not only for their beauty but for how they root faith in shared song. For some congregations, newer instruments and contemporary styles have been incorporated, creating vibrancy without displacing the richness of tradition.

Sometimes young and old have different needs. 'A lot of older people are not attracted to the noisy way of church,' another retired bishop tells me.

> They want the more quiet spirituality that has stood the test of time, with the familiar liturgy and hymns they know, while young people within our African tradition love the colour and flamboyancy of what we can offer; this is a way in which they feel they have a role and that they belong. A lot of people are attracted to a participatory style of worship which is not a one-person band.

Equally important is the church's holistic role in society. The experience of one leader is that our people are seeking moral as well as spiritual growth: 'In a world that has become disorderly and disjointed, people go to church because they long for ethical and moral guidance. They look for something that can provide structure, a more sustainable routine and purpose in their lives.' Another respondent adds, 'Listening to sermons gives me an insight as to how we should apply biblical principles in our lives.'

Living moral lives that reflect biblical principles is epitomised by the diocese of Eswatini, which is situated in South Africa's neighbouring country of that name. They frame their mission around five areas: Mission and Evangelism, Environment, Human Dignity, Sustainability and Anglican Identity.

The church speaks against injustice, advocates for the vulnerable and supports people seeking livelihoods. For many, this comprehensiveness – a faith that touches every part of life – is a key reason for remaining faithful. Within South Africa, our people believe we still have as important a role in defending and nurturing our new democracy as we did opposing apartheid. Writes one:

> We went through lots of trials and tribulations, and our hope was in God as it still is even now. Poor communities in rural areas, with first-hand experience of abject poverty, are often the strongest pillars of the Church. Like the poor widow, they give sacrificially because of their faith in him who, despite being rich, yet became poor for our sake. They don't rely on material means because they have none, but have God who is all in all as their only solace.

Elaborating, another bishop spells out the stark reality of a rural diocese with too few clergy:

> Most parishes consist of multiple congregations which do not see a priest every week and where a visit from the bishop is extremely rare. So it is up to the people, in the power of the Holy Spirit, to make church happen.

Week 2

Whether there is a priest or not, the people meet – and lay leaders see to the administration, lead Morning Prayer, preach, pray for the sick and visit those in need of special pastoral care. On a Sunday they expect to spend much of the day together. After the formal service, worshippers gather in their various organisations, and the church building and trees outside are dotted with meetings of the Mothers' Union, Anglican Women's Fellowship, youth groups, Men's Guilds and Bernand Mizeki Guild – each with its own particular focus and contribution to make to the life of the church.

In rural areas, church land and buildings become a valuable resource hub for the wider community, and parishes are encouraged to use their properties to serve their communities in activities such as growing vegetable gardens, housing homework clubs, running crèches for young children and hosting health clinics.

At the same time, people are clear about what must change. Young people in Taung voiced frustration that clergy sometimes hide behind rigid traditions rather than engage creatively. Our people call for stronger preaching, more pastoral care and a deeper inclusivity – particularly for those living with disability. Others long for revival services that rekindle faith, for lay-led Bible studies and devotions, and for a broader embrace of music that reflects the heart of today's communities. These are not complaints of people drifting away; they are the cries of people committed enough to want the church to thrive.

The underlying theme is clear: people attend because the church still matters to their lives. It is a place of encounter with God, a sanctuary from the world's noise, a family that sustains in hardship, a community that proclaims justice, and a fellowship where prayers are shared and answered. One voice captured it beautifully: 'As much joy as everything else in life brings me, coming to church brings me more. I find my peace at church, and it gives me a feeling of fulfilment.'

Reflection

For those of us in the Church of England, this Southern African witness is both a challenge and an encouragement. It challenges us to ask: do our churches provide safe spaces where people can encounter God afresh? Do we embody belonging in such a way that no one feels alone? Do our liturgies lead people to Christ with clarity and depth? Are we attentive to the voices of the young, who long not for entertainment but for meaningful participation?

And it encourages us with a reminder: decline is not the only story. Even in contexts where resources are few and challenges are many, people still gather — week by week, Sunday by Sunday — because they know that here they meet Christ, here they are restored, here they are not alone.

As Lent unfolds, may we learn from these testimonies. May we seek renewal not in programmes alone but in the living practices of worship, belonging and witness. May our parishes become places where life in all its fullness is celebrated, where burdens are shared, where youth and age alike find purpose, and where Christ remains at the centre. For wherever two or three gather in his name, there he is among them — still calling, still healing, still making all things new.

Following Christ in every season of life

The Most Revd Brian Williams, born in Buenos Aires, serves as the Anglican Bishop of Argentina and has held the role of Presiding Bishop of the Anglican Church of South America since 2023. Ordained in 1996 and consecrated as bishop in 2020, he previously ministered as rector of Iglesia de San Miguel y Todos los Ángeles, located on the outskirts of Buenos Aires. He is married to Verónica and together they have two sons.

A pastoral visit

One of the aspects I most treasure in my ministry is meeting people and having the privilege of speaking with them about the truly important matters of life. Visiting someone in their home is especially enriching because each house tells a lot about its residents, and people often feel more relaxed and open to sharing their stories.

It was mid-morning when I arrived at Susha's house. After a warm greeting, she asked me directly, 'What is the meaning of my life? What does God want from me?'

I've been asked these questions more than once, but this time felt different. Susha was 103 years old and had been bedridden for a year. Though she had almost completely lost her sight, her mental sharpness remained intact. She spoke five languages and, even at her advanced age, asked daily to be told the most important news from Argentina and around the world.

She had come to Buenos Aires from the Netherlands as a child and quickly learned Spanish. At the boarding school she attended, she became Anglican and encountered the love of Jesus. From that moment on, she served him with immense joy. But now, she struggled to see the purpose of remaining alive. She felt like a burden to her family and couldn't imagine how she might continue serving God as she had always done.

I knew that, behind her question, Susha was seeking an honest answer. She wasn't complaining about her physical condition; she genuinely wanted to understand why she was still here. Especially because she had always been a deeply generous and helpful person, and now she depended entirely on others.

I took her hand and said, 'First of all, thanks to you, the people who care for you receive a salary that helps them to support their families. You are a blessing to them. And beyond that, there is still much you can do to serve God.'

She listened intently to every word.

'You have time to pray for others, and that is incredibly important. Many people have little time to pray. You can pray for your family, for the Church, for me, for those who care for you, and for those who do not yet know the love of God. Use this time to pray. Use it to reflect on God's word and deepen your understanding of him. Share his love with those who visit you and those who attend to you. Use your time to listen, since people have a deep need to be heard, and you have the time and wisdom to listen and offer counsel.'

As I spoke, her face began to change, lighting up with a radiant smile. Then she said, 'Thank you. That's exactly what I needed to hear. I still have much to do for God.'

She paused, then added: 'Now tell me about your family, how are they?'

Reflection

> Peter began to say to him [Jesus], 'Look, we have left everything and followed you.'
> (Mark 10:28, NRSV)

Susha's story may prompt us to think of others who have become a source of wisdom and blessing in their later years. Such souls are a reminder that following Jesus is not a fleeting impulse: it is a lifelong posture. We follow him until our final breath.

To follow Jesus is to turn away from the world and walk with him. It is a choice each person must make freely, and it transforms the course of one's life.

The rich young man was unwilling to let go of his love for wealth, while Peter, the other disciples and millions throughout history have chosen otherwise. To walk with Jesus is to love him above all people and things, and to serve him with our whole being.

What is most precious is that this love and service can begin in early childhood and continue until our final day. It's a lifetime relationship with God.

Prayer

We thank you, Lord, for your immense love for us on the cross. That love moves us to love you unconditionally. Grant me the will to serve you throughout my life, so that others may also praise your holy name. Through Jesus Christ our Lord and Saviour. Amen.

Questions for reflection

1 What have you left – or what might you need to leave behind – to serve Jesus more fully?
2 In what ways are you currently serving him?
3 What aspects of your daily life could become opportunities to serve Jesus?

WEEK 3

A widow's might

Bishop Jo Bailey Wells is Deputy Secretary General of the Anglican Communion. Although she learned the faith from childhood, she credits formative experiences when she lived overseas as a young adult – in South Africa, Uganda, the USA, Mexico and Haiti – for waking her up to the radical implications of Jesus' love. Ordained in her late twenties, her ministry – mainly in teaching and training on three different continents – is regularly fuelled by the joy of encountering Christ in many different faces and cultures.

I was 18, relishing and risking the gift of a gap year spent seven thousand miles from home before university. I was posted to a former mission hospital in the rolling hills of Transkei, South Africa, working with the Pondo, a clan related to the Xhosa tribe. That region is breathtaking in its beauty, yet heartrending in its poverty.

In terms of language, culture, race and history the barriers were huge, yet the joy with which my fellow volunteer Barbara and I (*umlungu*, that is, white people) were received was remarkable. As was the faith of the Christians, who shone like beacons and lived their lives trusting God like I'd never seen before.

* * *

Week 3

I want to tell you about the most memorable day of a life-changing year. Many months in, when our conversational capacity in Xhosa had finally stretched beyond the simplest greetings, one of the mamas at church invited the two of us to visit her home.

'Walk in the direction of the sunset,' Nompendulo told us, pointing to the westerly horizon criss-crossed with footpaths.

The following weekend we set out, assisted by an impromptu gaggle of children serving as our guides. When we got there – 'there' being a compound consisting of a plot of maize and a single mud hut 'rondavel', furnished with a plastic chair and some rolled-up grass bedding mats – we were welcomed like royalty. Neighbours came to pay their respects, and we greeted dozens of friends and relatives. When the time came to eat, Nompendulo presented us with a steaming plate piled high with mealie meal, a few greens and some fried chicken. I confess it was a bit bony and tough but it was *meat*, a rare delicacy even back in the hospital where we stayed. Very uncomfortably, etiquette seemed to demand that others watched while we ate – even pressing us to have seconds – despite the crowd of hungry mouths surrounding us.

It wasn't until the walk home that Barbara and I had a chance to talk about what had happened. We spent the next week processing the experience. This was not a 'wealthy' compound where goats and hens strutted around. Where did our friend procure the food she served? Only later did we learn that she had slayed her one and only chicken – and this was in order to give us a feast, to offer us hospitality, to thank us for the 'honour' of visiting her home.

A widow's might

Truly, I realised, Nompendulo gave more than I could ever imagine giving. Here, before our eyes, was a replay of the widow Jesus observed at the Temple giving her two copper coins (Luke 21:1–4). When I give, it comes from the overflow of my abundance; but Nompendulo gave out of her poverty, quite literally the only meat she had.

Some of us may harbour questions about the wisdom of my friend's giving – after all, her children sorely needed that chicken so much more than Barbara and I did. Just as surely, the disciples might have queried why the widow gave her last pennies to the Temple treasury, of all places.

Both women held nothing back – in vulnerability and thanksgiving and faith – when surely they had multiple reasons not to do so. Life is fragile: won't this make it harder? Life is unjust: why be thankful in circumstances of politicised inequality and grinding poverty? Life is so uncertain: what if the deadly pestilence strikes home and family?

In the gospel, Jesus highlights the widow's commitment and its transforming power. His disciples already felt they had left everything to follow him, yet he points them to a woman – one of the poorest, perhaps one of the oldest, certainly one perceived to be the most 'power*less*' – and declares her not only a role model but the engine of true religion, of healthy Church. This passage is sometimes referred to as the widow and her mite – but I propose that the word should be spelled M-I-G-H-T.

The encounter with Nompendulo and others like her in Transkei challenged my own discipleship, and in hindsight I date the sense of call to ministry back to the privilege of this sojourn. Ever since, I've come to recognise generosity – to the point of sacrifice – as the most tangible signal of faithful discipleship, of a pure heart, of total following. It gets to the core of our being. What or who do we serve? What matters? And where is the evidence of our commitment?

Even writing such a thing leaves me nervous. And so, I ask myself: what do I fear? Do I suspect Jesus of a scam? Of luring me into poverty and destitution? In truth, he is offering a whole new world of abundance, of life at its richest and best.

This experience in South Africa – far away from home, outside my own cultural norms – was life-changing. Crudely, in my riches, I found myself *jealous* of those Xhosa people in their poverty – because they had a joy in life and a simplicity of living that I longed for. It turned my priorities upside down.

How I would love to find again that Xhosa mama whose life reshaped my life with a richer glimpse of abundance! Alas, she will never know the impact of her giving. Doubtless it's the same for the widow Jesus admired. And yet her actions – her whole-hearted whole-person whole-life giving – reveals to us the whole-hearted whole-person whole-life giving of the Saviour she follows. The Saviour who walks in the direction of the sunset to offer everything for us. And then returns again and again to find us, to eat with us, to transform our living and our giving … until, pray God, we become the sort of person through whom others may glimpse the beauty, the wholeness, the generosity of God. Who gives everything for each of us and all of us.

> And He looked up and saw the rich putting their gifts into the treasury, and He saw also a certain poor widow

putting in two mites. So He said, "Truly I say to you that this poor widow has put in more than all; for all these out of their abundance have put in offerings for God, but she out of her poverty put in all the livelihood that she had." (Luke 21:1–4, NKJV)

Prayer
Lord, I long to give myself more wholly to you. Transform the poverty of my nature by the riches of your grace, through Jesus Christ who gave everything. Amen.

Questions for reflection
1 Who do you know whose generosity amazes you? What is the impact of their giving?
2 Reflect on your own life: where are you rich and where are you poor?

Walking with the least

The Rt Revd David Eisho Uehara was born in August 1956 in Okinawa, Japan. He graduated from the Central Theological Seminary, Tokyo, in March 1986 and was appointed to the Church of St Peter and St Paul, Mihara, diocese of Okinawa, Nippon Sei Ko Kai (Anglican Church in Japan). Following this, David served at four other churches in Okinawa and also spent time at the Church Divinity School of the Pacific in California, USA, before being consecrated and installed as Bishop of the diocese of Okinawa in September 2013. He was installed as Primate of the Nippon Sei Ko Kai in May 2024.

The mission of the Anglican Church in Okinawa traces its roots to 1846, when Bernard Jean Bettelheim was sent by the British Royal Navy's Loochoo Mission to the Ryukyu islands. (These lie off the coast of Asia, forming a border between the East China Sea and the Philippine Sea.) However, under Japan's prohibition of Christianity, his work bore little fruit. In 1894, following Japan's victory in the Sino-Japanese War, Okinawa was formally annexed. Missionaries were then dispatched from the Kyushu diocese, but no self-supporting church was established.

In the early Shōwa period, which began in 1926, Dr Hannah Riddell, Director of Kaishun Hospital in Kumamoto, Kyushu, sent the Japanese Christian missionary, Mr Keisai Aoki, who suffered from leprosy, to Okinawa, for the sake of evangelism and care. At that time, discrimination, prejudice and persecution against people with leprosy were severe. Mr Aoki visited people with leprosy who were living in caves by the sea or in makeshift huts in the mountains, tending their wounds and sharing the gospel, and from these small gatherings, a Christian community slowly emerged. The facility established by Mr Aoki and his companions was later transferred to the government, becoming the National Sanatorium Okinawa Airaku-en. Thus, the Anglican mission in Okinawa was born from among those who had leprosy.

Soon after, however, in 1941, the Pacific War broke out, and Okinawa became the site of a devastating ground battle in which more than 200,000 lives were lost. Many civilians perished, some massacred by the Japanese army, others forced into collective suicide. After the war, Okinawa was held under US military occupation and cut off from mainland Japan. Land was confiscated from residents to build massive bases, which became launching points for later wars in Korea, Vietnam and the Gulf. Under the San Francisco Peace Treaty, Okinawa was separated from Japan.

In 1949, Bishop Hinsuke Yashiro, a prominent figure in the Anglican Church in Japan, attended the General Convention of the Episcopal Church in the United States and appealed for pastoral care for Mr Aoki and his community at Okinawa Airaku-en. Postwar mission in Okinawa was thus carried out by American Episcopalians, leading to the founding of nine congregations, beginning with the House of Prayer at Airaku-en, with Okinawa in time becoming a missionary diocese of The Episcopal Church.

In 1972, after a long struggle and widespread protests against US occupation, Okinawa was returned to Japan, and the diocese of Okinawa was established. Yet to this day, vast US military bases remain, and incidents, accidents and crimes connected to them continue to afflict the people of that region.

From this history, two prayers arise from the diocese of Okinawa:

- that all prejudice and discrimination are eliminated, and everyone may be free to live with dignity;
- that military bases may disappear, and a truly peaceful world may come.

Our Lord Jesus said:

'Truly, I say to you, as you did it to one of the least of these my brothers and sisters, you did it to me.'
(Matthew 25:40, ESV, adapted)

The diocese of Okinawa, the smallest in the Nippon Sei Ko Kai, longs to follow the example of Jesus and walk alongside those who have been diminished or marginalised by society.

Renewing our baptismal covenant as a Lenten practice

The Rt Revd Dr DeDe Duncan-Probe is Diocesan Bishop of the Episcopal diocese of Central New York, where she has been blessed to serve with God's faithful people since 2016.

Lent is a season of prayer, fasting and self-examination. Jesus' time in the desert serves as an ideal model for us. In fact, we often refer to Lent as a season apart, our own desert time preparing us for the resurrection of Jesus Christ. And yet in my ministry context, it is our separation that is hindering our relationship with God, our neighbours and our own souls.

In 2023, the Surgeon General of the United States declared a state of emergency due to the epidemic of loneliness and isolation sweeping our country. With the impact on mental and physical health on a par with the dangers of smoking, harmful societal isolation has increased rates of depression and anxiety and, perhaps most shockingly, seen an almost 30 per cent rise in premature mortality, heart disease, stroke and dementia. In 2024, the American Psychiatric Association published a poll in which 1 in 3 Americans (across all age groups) stated that they feel lonely every week.

The diocese of Central New York is a largely agricultural area, and in our context, the effects of isolation and loneliness challenge every aspect of our diocesan ministry. In our post-Covid reality, people remain hesitant to gather socially, our civic communities are deeply divided by political tribalism, and our seeking after justice and dignity is often perceived as too political. As a diocesan bishop, I regularly receive complaints regarding clergy sermons and diocesan ministries, citing political bias. These challenges are not unique; the devastating effects of isolation and loneliness are a worldwide issue, a worldwide *spiritual* issue.

In the Anglican Communion, the covenant we make at baptism, a liturgical expression of the Apostle's Creed, is our foundational response to God and to one another as God's people. Put in a different way, we have vowed to be God's people in community and to continue the work of the apostles. It is worth noting that the fourth bidding of our baptismal covenant asks, 'Will you continue in the apostle's teaching, in the fellowship, in the breaking of bread and in the prayers?' In other words, will we continue to be a dynamic community of faith? And we respond that, with God's help, we will.

When I make pastoral visits to the parishes of our diocese, renewing our baptismal covenant is a liturgical part of our worship. So, prior to worship, when I meet with those who will be baptised, confirmed or received, I ask what has brought them to this profession of faith, and what they are hoping will change as a result. Amid the varied responses I have heard over the years, a constant theme expressed is a desire for deeper community and connection. I then go on to highlight the pivotal moment in the liturgy, and all who are gathered respond that, on behalf of God's Church, they will support 'these persons in their life of faith'. All of us need to know that

Renewing our baptismal covenant as a Lenten practice

our community of faith supports us and walks with us in our vulnerability and in our strength, and to be reminded that our faith is communal and relational.

In 1 Corinthians 12:12–13 (NRSV), the Apostle Paul tells us,

> For just as the body is one and has many members, and all the members of the body, though many, are one body, so it is with Christ. For in the one Spirit we were all baptized into one body.

In our baptismal vows, this understanding is echoed as we have covenanted with God to be the body of Christ, to grow in our faith, and to seek to serve and love our neighbours as ourselves. Working for justice and the dignity of all God's creation is more than a good idea; we have vowed to God that we will pursue this faith.

So perhaps this Lent is an opportunity to see our piety with new eyes, with open hearts to the reality of our being the body of Christ. In addition to our usual prayer and fasting, this may be a time for renewed commitment to sacred gathering, to caring for the lost, the isolated and the lonely, perhaps including ourselves. As people of God, we need one another; we are incomplete without one another. I pray that the Holy Spirit will rekindle our first love and renew a fire within our hearts as God's beloved people. Together, let us walk from isolation to fellowship, from injustice to justice, from loneliness to community, and continue in the apostles' teaching and fellowship, in the breaking of bread and in the prayers. May the redeeming love of Jesus Christ guide our journey this holy season.

Prayer

Grant, O God, that your holy and life-giving Spirit may so move every human heart [and especially the hearts of the people of this land], that barriers which divide us may crumble, suspicions disappear, and hatreds cease; that our divisions being healed, we may live in justice and peace; through Jesus Christ our Lord. Amen.

(Prayer for Social Justice, Book of Common Prayer)

Questions for reflection

1 In what ways do isolation and loneliness have an impact on your life and faith?
2 In I Corinthians 12:12–17, what does it mean to you that you are essential to the body of Christ, and what might help you to live more fully into this relationship with God's community?
3 As you consider the baptismal covenant, what things might you be called to repent of or to embrace in your own life of faith?

Discipleship as relationships

The Revd Canon Sammy Wainaina serves as the Adviser to the Archbishop of Canterbury on Anglican Communion Affairs. His ministry takes him across many parts of the Anglican Communion – from bustling cities to remote villages – where he encounters real people walking with Jesus in diverse, often challenging contexts. These experiences continually deepen his faith and remind him of the beauty and resilience of discipleship lived out in everyday life. It's not always polished. It's often quiet, sometimes costly, but always deeply rooted in love for Jesus.

The Mango Tree Church

In a dusty village in northern Uganda, I once sat under a mango tree with a congregation whose church building had been destroyed during conflict. There were no pews, no altar, no roof – just people, Scripture and song. An elderly woman named Mama Grace stood to testify. She had lost her son in the violence. Her home had been burned. Yet she said, 'I follow Jesus because he sat with me in the ashes. When I had nothing, he gave me peace.' Her words have never left me. They were not dramatic, but they were true. In that moment, I saw discipleship not as a doctrine, but as a relationship. Christ was not just preached – he was present. And in that presence, we find the heartbeat of the Anglican Communion: a shared faith that walks with people in every context, every language, every landscape.

Discipleship across the Communion

In South Sudan, we met a young priest who leads worship under a tree because his church too was destroyed in conflict. He said, 'We don't need walls to meet Jesus. He walks with us here.'

In the Solomon Islands, we joined a community where the gospel is sung in native languages, echoing through the rainforest.

In England, we sat with a group of asylum seekers who found healing in the liturgy and welcome in the Eucharist.

These stories remind us that discipleship is not confined to geography or tradition. It is a living response to the presence of Christ – whether in lament or celebration, in silence or song.

Testimonies that inspire

I think of Daniel, a young man who came to faith after attending a youth camp. He had grown up in silence and sorrow. But at camp, he heard the story of the Prodigal Son. He wept. 'I didn't know God was waiting for me,' he said.

Today, Daniel leads a small fellowship at his university. He preaches, prays and mentors others. His life is a testimony – not just of conversion, but of transformation.

Discipleship as relationships

I also think of Agnes, a widow who started a prayer group in her home. She couldn't read, but she could pray. Her group grew into a vibrant house church. 'I may not know many words,' she said, 'but I know Jesus walks with me.'

Why we follow

People across the Communion follow Christ for many reasons:

- **because he is present in suffering**: in places of war, displacement and poverty, Jesus is not a distant figure – he is the companion in the fire;
- **because he brings joy**: in dance, in song, in shared meals, discipleship is often expressed through celebration;
- **because he calls us to justice**: in contexts of inequality, discipleship becomes a prophetic witness – speaking truth, defending the vulnerable and embodying hope.

Scripture that resonates

But now thus says the LORD,
    he who created you, O Jacob,
    he who formed you, O Israel:
Do not fear, for I have redeemed you;
    I have called you by name, you are
        mine.
(Isaiah 43:1, NRSV)

This verse echoes across cultures. In Uganda, it's sung in choirs. In Pakistan, it's whispered in prayer. In Wales, it's read at baptisms. It reminds us that discipleship begins not with our effort, but with God's initiative. We are named. We are known. We are his.

Prayer
Lord Jesus, you walk with us in every place – in joy and sorrow, in strength and weakness. Teach us to follow you with courage, to share your love with boldness, and to celebrate your presence in every corner of the Communion. Amen.

Questions for reflection
1 Where have you seen Christ walking with people in unexpected places?
2 What story from your own journey might encourage someone else to follow Jesus?
3 How can your local church reflect the global heartbeat of discipleship?

When there are no words to pray

The Most Revd Shane Parker was born to Irish parents in Edmonton, Alberta, and lived in western Canada during his childhood. He worked as a labourer for several years before studying to become a professional sociologist. After studies in theology, Shane served as a parish priest, diocesan archdeacon, cathedral dean and bishop in the diocese of Ottawa prior to his election as Primate of All Canada in 2025. He and his wife Katherine have three adult children and three grandchildren. He enjoys physical work and is most comfortable in natural places.

Let me take you to a quintessentially Canadian place not too far from Ottawa, the country's capital city. I would like to describe a disconcerting spiritual experience many people will recognise – no matter where you live in the Anglican Communion – and to offer a word of hope.

There are 800 hectares of forest in the Gatineau Hills of Western Québec. Over thirty years ago, while serving as the incumbent of a parish, I lived on the edge of this forest for five years, and I've spent many hours there since. It is a place of deep familiarity and comfort.

Week 3

There are no official points of interest in this part of the Gatineaus and, until recently, no marked trails. The forest is bordered by three roads, giving it an elongated triangular shape. The roadways have no places to park, serving mostly to get people to other destinations, which means that only a few human beings tend to be in the forest at any one time.

Wildlife sightings are common, and I have frequently encountered evidence of deer, porcupine, bear, fisher, weasel, rabbit and other small rodents – including flying squirrels. There are also many birds, big and small, hunters and hunted, and lots of woodpeckers – especially the large and noisy Pileated Woodpecker. After a snowfall, it's a joy to follow the trails left in the snow by forest creatures, simply to see where they lead …

There are steep cliffs and a ridge that climbs 820 feet (250 metres) along the eastern section of the forest before winding its way, broken by a creek valley, down to the southern point of the triangle. When the wind comes from the east, this unprotected ridge (should you have made the not inconsiderable effort of clambering up there) can feel very cold indeed, with snow forming into deep drifts and crevasses.

There is a substantial pond in the central part of the forest, nestled between the tall peaks and the ridge to the east, and the round, undulating hills to the north and west. The pond flows eastwards over a robust beaver dam and forms into a brook, twisting its way through a marshy area before trickling down into a subterranean passageway. Steep drops and crags make it difficult to trace its pathway from there, so that the portal where the water disappears seems kind of mystical – the sort of place you feel ought to be named after a Celtic saint.

When there are no words to pray

To the west of this large pond is a tall, graceful white pine, which stands alone. Every time I return, I visit this old friend, who has silently listened to the cares of my heart over the years. I call it the Vigil Tree.

The Vigil Tree keeps watch over the sanctuary of the forest. It appears to know that our prayers cannot always be put into words. Some things feel too big or complicated or harrowing to express that way. Sometimes we are in pain, or fearful, or fallen or famished in body or spirit. Sometimes there is nothing to say, nothing to offer, nothing but emptiness – even as we long for God's grace.

The Vigil Tree seems to embody the words of Paul, who taught that when we cannot pray ourselves, the Holy Spirit prays for us, interceding 'with sighs too deep for words' (Romans 8:26, NRSV).

Sometimes it is enough to go to a place that is familiar and safe, be it a forest, a church, a window or even a place in your mind, and to open your heart to God – wordlessly. And God, who searches your heart, will hear the prayer of the Spirit within you.

WEEK 4

Giving your faith for others

The Most Revd Dr Maimbo Mndolwa is Diocesan Bishop of Tanga, which is among the 28 dioceses of the Anglican Church of Tanzania. He is also Archbishop of Tanzania.

Tanzania, and Tanga in particular, is a multi-religious region, where Christians, Muslims and African religions coexist peacefully. Although adherents of these religions occasionally find it difficult to convert from one faith to another, it is relatively easy for Christians to become Muslims.

The story of Neema (not her real name) is an illustration of this. She was born and baptised in the Anglican Church but later married to a devout Muslim at Negero village. Until the Government outed it, this village was a strong base of Alkhaida, one of the Islamic militant groups from Somalia.

My first visit to Negero church to carry out confirmations took place in April 2012. (In fact, it was the first episcopal visit since the church's establishment in the 1990s.) By then, Neema was a very popular ward councillor in the area. I confirmed her and she promised to assist the church in the process of acquiring more land, a promise she fulfilled within two years. This made it possible to construct a permanent church building. When I visited again in 2015, I asked Neema about the whereabouts of her husband and family.

She told me they were all Muslims, and her husband would not allow their children to accompany her to church services.

I probed more. 'May I see him after the Mass?'

'No!' she responded.

When I visited the church a year later, Neema told me that she had converted to Islam. I was angry but could not get her to change her mind. After the Mass we sat and talked, and in the course of deep conversation, she finally divulged that she had a mission which she would not reveal to anyone until it matured. I left Negero with an aching heart, feeling we had lost a 'big sheep'. It was unfortunate that I was unable to return to the village the following year, when I'd planned to meet Neema again, but in 2018, the year I was made Archbishop, a visit again became possible.

It was 8.30 a.m. when I arrived at Negero, and Neema was standing at the entrance to the churchyard. She waved and I asked my driver to stop in response.

When I got out of the car, she grabbed my hand and said, 'Bishop, I have a gift for the church and for you.'

I asked her to give it to me and I would deliver it to the church.

'No!' she replied, 'I will do it by myself during the Mass.'

I said, '*Vyedi*' ('OK' in Zigua, her tribal language).

We began the Mass, but before I had concluded my homily, she came forward. 'I have a confession to make and a gift to present.'

I almost fainted, thinking she was going to reveal how harsh I had been about her sin of converting to Islam. But instead, we received a true gift from God: her husband and his seven children and her five in-laws were in the church, pleading for baptism.' What a harvest,' I whispered.

Neema told me, 'Bishop, this was what I wanted to do, and I thank God for his mercy that I have been able to do it. So, please baptise them and confirm them.' I called for the book of canon law to see if there was any rubric to guide me. I found one stating that a new convert from Islam needs at least six months of continuous teaching before baptism.

While I was asking myself how my Cathedral Chapter and the House of Bishops would respond if I went ahead, Neema said, 'Bishop, before baptising them, please give me absolution from my sin, so that after baptism and confirmation you can bless our marriage.'

I quickly pulled off my cope and mitre and went into the vestry, picked up my purple stole and asked her to kneel down so that the rite she requested could be completed. When I came back, I called for water for baptism, confirmed the family and then blessed Neema's marriage. I have never since experienced such a joyful church service!

Suppose you were Neema. Would you dare to put your faith at such risk? I doubt it. I also wonder how you would have handled Neema's case if you'd been me? Matthew 10:9 tells us that, since Christian faith is granted to us freely, it has to be passed to others for free. This free gift is grace, and the Kiwahili word for grace is actually the name I gave to the dear soul in my story, *'neema'*. It is a free gift because of its nature: 'a divine favour and blessing from God'.

Our canon laws, Prayer Book rubrics and personal attitudes can sometimes push people away from God instead of drawing them in. Although it is true that without canon laws and rubrics the church can become a chaotic institution, we also need to remember that the Holy Spirit is more powerful than written law. Just consider the story of Peter and Cornelius in Acts.10:1 – 11:18 and how the position of the early church was challenged by the Holy Spirit.

St Augustine wrote, 'Our hearts are restless until they find their rest in you.' In Matthew 28:18–20, our Lord commanded us to go and make disciples. St Augustine's words remind us that every Christian is given a specific unshakable longing to carry out this great commission. Although our contexts differ, my prayer during this fourth week of Lent is that our hearts would not find rest until we have given our faith to other people, even if we're prompted to do so in ways some may not understand. Amen.

'Not my will but yours be done'

The Rt Revd Anthony Ball is Director of the Anglican Centre in Rome and the Archbishop of Canterbury's Representative to the Holy See. He was born in Africa, educated principally in England, and ordained while serving in HM Diplomatic Service. He subsequently worked at Lambeth Palace before becoming a parish priest in Sussex and then a Canon of Westminster. While at Westminster Abbey, he also served as a bishop in the Province of Alexandria, latterly as Bishop in North Africa.

Me?

Life (or at least mine) is full of 'who would have thought?' moments. I experienced one of these as I was standing on the roof of the clergy house building in Cairo, looking across at the distinctive architecture of All Saints' Cathedral where I was soon to be consecrated as bishop. Twenty-five years earlier, as a young diplomat living in Egypt to learn Arabic, the gentle encouragement of the then Deacon Munir Sostanees had helped me to reconnect with my calling. Mouneer died young and never knew what an influence he had on my faith journey. The evenings we spent reading the Bible in Arabic together (or at least trying to – I was never a great linguist!), and the vision he shared of ministry and discipleship, prompted me to begin going to church regularly again. A quarter of a century later, Munir's brother-in-law was about to be the principal consecrator at my episcopal ordination. Who would have thought?

Responding to a call

I had long sensed a strange interior tug towards 'church service' (no more clearly defined than that) but had rejected the idea of ordination as incompatible with my hopes for a career and comfortable lifestyle. God had other plans! As I've often found, I was led gently towards (what I take to be) a realisation of those plans after being obedient to that 'tug' and the promptings of faithful people around me.

First came ordination alongside my secular career, then stipendiary ministry and now, seemingly full circle, a role combining ministry and diplomacy. At each stage, there were those whose own lives were an inspiration and an encouragement that, however inadequate or anxious I might feel about stepping out in response to my perception of God's call, it would be possible. So, for me, being a disciple has meant being obedient to what I discerned as God's will. It has involved trusting that there is a purpose behind the different opportunities I have had and the circumstances I have faced, and that it was for my good – even, or perhaps especially, when that was not obvious. Often 'the plan', and the joy that derives from having followed it, only becomes apparent in the rear-view mirror. Now, with a few more miles on the clock, part of my discipleship is trying to help others discern God's will for them, to help them know – in the words of Augustine of Hippo (whose

'Not my will but yours be done'

first Anglican successor I was to become) that 'our hearts are restless until they find their rest in you'.

Sacrifice

I regularly include in my own prayers the words Jesus prayed shortly before his arrest and passion – 'not my will but yours be done' (Luke 22:42, NRSV). It is not easy to put that prayer into practice (indeed, what followed for Jesus was making the ultimate sacrifice). For while the Bible points us to God's will in a general sense, discerning what that might be at an individual level or at a particular time in our lives is complex and sometimes uncertain. Should we manage to clear that hurdle, it can then be difficult to come to terms with any sacrifices (money, time, security and so on) demanded. I was already an ordinand when my wife and I got married, and I was already ordained when our son was born, so I'm well aware of the effect that making sacrifices can have on others. Yet, it is often through what feels like the hardest elements of Christian discipleship that the greatest fulfilment seems to come.

Being with Jesus

Dr Rowan Williams, whom I served for six years when he was Archbishop of Canterbury, published a wonderful little book, *Being Disciples,* which I thoroughly recommend. He observes that, in the ancient world, being the student or disciple of a master was not a matter of turning up to lectures and jotting down notes; it was more like sitting at the master's feet, sleeping outside his door and hanging on his every word: 'It's not an intermittent state; it's a relationship that continues.'[1] The Gospels describe Jesus' disciples travelling with him, observing him, obeying him, talking among themselves and sometimes sharing in his ministry. He often takes them to unexpected and uncomfortable places.

Through reading the Bible, prayer and discussion with others, we can seek to discover where Jesus would be in the daily life of our world, try to join him there and encourage others to do the same.

I vividly sensed Christ one day as I was confirming dozens of people in a mud church in a refugee camp in Ethiopia; my perception of his presence was no less twenty-four hours later, during Choral Evensong in Westminster Abbey.

A meditation

In November 2025, I attended the wonderful service in which Pope Leo made John Henry Newman a Doctor of the Universal Church. Newman's Anglican and Roman Catholic writings were both celebrated, and I end with an extract from a meditation that strikes me as being as true today as when Newman wrote it on 7 March 1848:

> God has created me to do Him some definite service; He has committed some work to me which He has not committed to another ... Somehow I am necessary for His purposes ... I am a link in a chain, a bond of connexion between persons ... if I do but keep His commandments and serve Him in my calling.[2]

'Not my will but yours be done'

Questions for reflection
1 Look back at your life so far. Are there moments or experiences that you now recognise as equipping you for some service to your 'neighbour'? Is there a sense that this was God's will?
2 How do you feel about sharing your experience of being a disciple with others? Have you ever done that with someone you've only recently met or outside a church-related context?

The expanse of the thin veil

The Rt Revd Helen Kennedy was born and raised in England, emigrating to the Canadian Prairies over twenty-five years ago. Helen studied theological education in Winnipeg, Manitoba, while working in youth ministry and raising a family. After ordination, she was a priest in Winnipeg for fifteen years before being elected to the Episcopate for the diocese of Qu'Appelle in 2021. Helen is married with grown children, and her passions include riding motorcycle and quilting (though not at the same time).

There's a well-worn joke in Saskatchewan: 'It's so flat here that you can see your dog run away for two days.' This lighthearted banter nearly always gets a smile, yet beneath the humour lies a deeper truth about the vastness of this land.

In Genesis 1:6–8, God creates an 'expanse' (rā·qî·a'/רְקִיעַ) – a firmament – to divide the waters above from the waters below. This image of divine separation of the celestial and terrestrial gives order and shape to our world. Here on the Prairies, that expanse is something we know intimately. It shapes our imaginations and our faith; it stretches our sense of perspective and mirrors something of the infinite nature of God.

The Canadian Prairies – often called the 'breadbasket of the world' – encompass more than 150 million acres of farmland that helps to feed the globe. Yet, their richness is not only agricultural. Over millennia, the land has been sculpted by ice and time into valleys, rivers and wide-open plains. Under the immense 360-degree horizon, heaven and earth meet, demanding our attention. The 'Land of Living Skies', as Saskatchewan is known, displays heaven in the song and shimmer of the Northern Lights and in sunsets that seem to set the whole world aflame. In this wide and wondrous space, the veil between the earthly and the divine feels remarkably thin. As we look across fields of wheat, canola, flax or lentils, creation itself seems to lean toward heaven. Each sweeping view, each rustling breeze, carries a whisper of the sacred. This 'holy nearness' lies at the very heart of Lent; a season whose sole purpose is to deepen our awareness of God's presence in our midst.

For all its beauty, the Prairie landscape can also be unforgiving. Winter lingers long here; wind scours the horizon clean; fields lie empty beneath endless skies. Yet this very starkness becomes a teacher. Lent draws us into such places of bareness – not to punish or diminish us, but to strip away what is unnecessary, that we might rediscover what truly sustains. The wilderness is never wasted ground. In Scripture, it is the place where God's people encounter truth. It is where Israel learned to trust the manna of grace over the certainty of slavery, and where Jesus faced both temptation and affirmation: 'You are my beloved.' The wilderness is where our illusions unravel and our dependence upon God becomes real. Prairie landscapes teach us this truth. Out here, the horizon refuses to be ignored. There is nowhere to hide, nothing to distract us from the slow, honest work of watching and waiting. Lent asks of us that same attentiveness: to listen and look, to let the vastness humble and transform us.

When the snow still lies thick and the soil sleeps, it can be hard to imagine that anything is happening beneath the surface. Life waits patiently underground, gathering strength for spring. So too, in our Lenten wilderness, God works unseen – softening the frozen ground of our hearts, preparing us for the season of resurrection.

On the Prairies, we know that transformation comes slowly. The thaw begins not with spectacle, but with subtle signs – the trickle of meltwater, the return of migrating geese whose calls echo through the open sky. Then, almost suddenly, life bursts forth. The fields awaken, goslings appear, and starkness is replaced by abundance.

This is the rhythm of resurrection: quiet beginnings, steady emergence, then unexpected joy. The wilderness gives way to the garden. Death yields to life.

Our spiritual lives, too, move through seasons of cold and thaw, of silence and song. Lent is not an end unto itself, but a passage. We are not meant to stay in the wilderness for ever, but to pass through it with hearts open and expectant – to see that what once seemed lifeless is now pulsing with new creation.

As God renews the land, so God renews the Church. Just as the light dances across the fields, so too grace moves among us, gently nudging us toward growth and reconciliation. In both rural parishes and bustling city congregations, in multi-point ministries and within the arches of our cathedral, we are called to be signs of renewal – communities where inclusion

The expanse of the thin veil

is not just an ideal but a lived reality. In a place where creativity flourishes, we will be released to face challenges together, united in prayer and discernment.

When we live like this – when we bless rather than judge, forgive rather than divide, and include rather than exclude – we make resurrection visible. We 'thin the veil' between heaven and earth, showing that the kingdom of God is not a distant dream, but a living reality breaking forth here and now, beneath these same wide skies.

Lent, like the Prairie winter, can feel bleak and unending. But Easter always comes. May we embrace the openness of our surroundings and let it teach us how to live with openness of spirit. May we cultivate hearts wide enough to hold the world, and eyes attentive enough to see God at work in all creation. The fields will green again. The light will return. And in the wide, living sky, the promise of resurrection will once more unfold.

Prayer

Creator God,
you have written your grace across the
    face of the land
and set your promise in the living skies.
In our seasons of wilderness,
open our hearts to the working of your
    Spirit.
Lead us through bleakness towards the
    joy of resurrection.
May your Spirit move through the wide
    expanse of our lives,

thinning the veil between heaven and
>   earth,
until all creation is renewed in your light
>   and love;
through Jesus Christ our Lord.
Amen.

Questions for reflection

1 How does the vastness and openness of the Prairie landscape I've described help you reflect on your own spiritual journey, especially during seasons that feel barren or challenging?
2 In what ways have 'wilderness' experiences in your life (times of waiting, emptiness, or uncertainty) helped to deepen your awareness of God's presence and grace?
3 How might you embody the 'spaciousness' described in the text within your own community, making it a place of renewal, inclusion and transformation?

'The kingdom of God is in your midst'

The Most Revd Stephen Than Myint Oo is Archbishop of Myanmar and Bishop of Yangon.

'The kingdom of God is in your midst.'
(Luke 17:21, NIV)

'Whoever wants to be my disciple must deny themselves and take up their cross and follow me.'
(Matthew 16:24, NIV)

Opening prayer

Lord Jesus,
you said that your kingdom is in our
    midst — not distant, but near.
As we journey through this Lenten season,
    open our eyes to see your presence
in the midst of our struggles and our
    service.
May your kingdom come through our faith,
    our love and our daily obedience.
Amen.

Week 4

A shepherd's reflection

When I look back on recent years in Myanmar – through the long nights of the COVID-19 pandemic and the pain of the military coup – I see more clearly than ever what it means to follow Jesus as his disciple. It was a time filled with uncertainty and grief. Yet in those dark valleys, I witnessed the quiet power of God's kingdom alive among his people.

During the pandemic, our churches were closed, our streets silent and our people afraid. But even behind locked doors, faith did not die. Families gathered around open Bibles at home. Neighbours shared rice and medicine. Pastors and laypeople found ways to bring encouragement by phone or by prayer. One day, as I read the words of Jesus – 'The kingdom of God is in your midst' – it struck me: the Church was still alive, vibrant and faithful, even in silence. The kingdom of God was not somewhere else; it was here, in the compassion and courage of his disciples.

Finding God in the midst of suffering

When the coup struck in 2021, our nation was shaken once again. Fear and sorrow returned with new force. People fled their homes; many were displaced or separated from their families. Yet even then, God's presence never left us.

I remember visiting a small congregation in a remote conflict-torn area. They had lost everything, yet they gathered under a bamboo roof to sing hymns and share the Lord's

'The kingdom of God is in your midst'

Supper. Their faith humbled me. One mother told me, 'Archbishop, we have nothing left but Christ – and he is enough.'

In that moment, I felt as if heaven had touched earth. Christ was present in their worship, in their tears, in their hope. The kingdom of God was truly in our midst.

Discipleship in the midst of the kingdom

Discipleship is not about comfort but about faithfulness. Jesus never promised us safety, but he promised his presence. To follow him is to carry our cross and to live out his love wherever we are placed.

- **Discipleship means perseverance**
  Faith grows deeper in adversity. The storms of life do not destroy true disciples; they refine them.
- **Discipleship means service**
  We follow Christ best when we serve others – feeding the hungry, healing the wounded, comforting the grieving.
- **Discipleship means hope**
  Even when the world trembles, disciples carry hope that the risen Christ reigns and his kingdom is breaking through.
- **Discipleship means community**
  No one walks alone. In times of isolation, we rediscover fellowship – praying together, encouraging one another and training new leaders for the future Church.

Week 4

The kingdom that is here – and coming

The British theologian N. T. Wright often reminds us that Jesus did not speak of the kingdom as a distant reward after death, but as God's rule breaking into the present world. Heaven and earth are not separate realities; they are destined to be renewed together when Christ returns. Every act of faith, love and justice today is a sign of that coming renewal – a glimpse of the new heaven and new earth God will one day reveal in fullness.

This is why I believe the kingdom of God is not far from us. It is already here, quietly transforming hearts and communities. Every prayer, every act of forgiveness, every moment of compassion are part of that kingdom work. Even in the midst of suffering, God is preparing his new creation – and we, his disciples, are invited to join him in that holy labour.

Hope for the journey

As I reflect on the challenges of these years, I am filled not with despair but with hope. For wherever people follow Christ in humility and courage, the kingdom is near. It is among the poor who share their last meal, the peacemakers who reconcile neighbours, and the faithful who keep believing when the world says otherwise.

The storms may rage, but Christ still reigns. His kingdom cannot be shaken. And one day, as N. T. Wright reminds us, heaven and earth will finally be one – when God renews all things and dwells fully among his people. Until that glorious day, we are called to live as citizens of that kingdom here and now, bearing its light in a darkened world.

Prayer

Lord Jesus,
your kingdom is already here, though not
    yet complete.
Strengthen us to follow you faithfully,
to serve with love,
and to hope with courage.
As we carry our crosses,
may we see glimpses of your glory
    breaking into our world.
Amen.

Questions for reflection

1. Where have I seen signs of God's kingdom in the midst of my own trials?
2. How can I make Christ's love visible in my community this week?
3. What small act of service can reflect God's renewing work on earth?

WEEK 5

A compelling community

The Rt Revd Anashuya Fletcher is a Sri Lankan-born bishop in the Anglican Church in Aotearoa New Zealand and Polynesia, serving as Assistant Bishop in the Anglican diocese of Wellington. Throughout her life, Bishop Anashuya has discovered sweet spots where the way God has made and called her meets the deep needs of our world – as a church planter, lawyer, baker, missional leader and social entrepreneur – and she loves helping others to discover the same in their own lives.

Many years ago, our family connected with another family whose children attended the same preschool. Although my husband and I were in local ministry, we had never had a faith conversation with this family. Then one day after a significant life crisis, the husband underwent a dramatic conversion experience through an encounter with some street evangelists, and the whole family showed up at a service. As our friendship grew, we began to learn more about what was happening in one another's lives. These new friends of ours had big, complex stories that meant they carried deep wounds and pain. They slowly opened up to us and allowed us the privilege of journeying with them through some of the hardest moments of their lives: relationship breakdowns; debilitating mental health episodes; past history catching up; wider family conflict.

Week 5

For many years, the complexities of their circumstances meant that they would dip in and out of the church community, yet they would always return. Through it all they were sustained by the endless grace and unbounded love of Christ; there was also something profoundly compelling about this compassionate community of Jesus' followers that called them back into a place of deep belonging.

Our family shifted from that community a while ago. Recently, however, I attended an event at the church and was surprised when I bumped into the mum. Here she was, part of the hospitality team – serving, contributing and hosting others. Her whole being radiated a confidence and non-anxious presence. It's hard to overstate the contrast with the woman we met years go. She is a living testament to the slow but miraculous transforming power of God in her life.

Here in Aotearoa New Zealand, we've heard anecdotally of a fresh wave of the Spirit at work, drawing people through the doors of our churches. People are literally walking in off the street. A key question for our time is what (or perhaps more importantly, who) will they find inside those doors?

When I reflect on this family's journey, central to their story of faith is the compelling nature of the community they found themselves a part of. A community comprising people who might not otherwise have shared a room with one another, but who were brought together by Christ's reconciling work of making family. A community whose care and compassion tangibly expressed God's boundless love and grace. A community that walked with them through the valley of the shadow of death, reminding them in practical ways of God's presence.

A compelling community

The husband's dramatic conversion on the street was only the beginning. Someone had the courage to share the gospel with a stranger – someone planted a seed – but it took years of faithful tending by others for that seed to bear fruit. In a culture that prizes immediacy and visible success, the Church's willingness to walk with people through their mess and pain towards healing and transformation remains one of the most powerful witnesses to the gospel. Miraculous transformation happens in both a moment and through the long, faithful, loving presence of ordinary disciples in one another's lives.

As we consider what people will find when they step through our church doors today, may we aspire to be that kind of compelling community. The Spirit continues to draw people in, but it is often the love and life of Christ expressed through those within the church that helps them to remain. May we, too, be a people whose lives radiate transforming grace – a community where the hurting find hope, the lost find belonging, and all of us together are continually being renewed by the love of God.

Prayer

Loving and gracious God, we thank you that through your Spirit you draw us together as one.

Empower us by that same Spirit to reflect your love to friend, foe and stranger alike.

Continue your transforming work within us, that we may become a compelling community – a living witness to the love, hope, joy and newness of life found only in you.

We ask this through Jesus Christ our Lord. Amen.

Week 5

Questions for reflection
1 What kind of community is being cultivated in your church?
2 When have you witnessed the slow, steady work of God's grace in a person's life, and how might that shape the way you accompany others in faith?
3 If someone 'walked in off the street' today, what would they encounter in you – and in us together – that reflects the love and life of Christ?

'My Lord and My God': confessing Christ amid trials

The Most Revd B. K. Nayak is Moderator, Synod of the Church of North India (CNI).

> Thomas responded to him, 'My Lord and my God!'
> (John 20:28, CSB)

> If you confess with your mouth, 'Jesus is Lord,' and believe in your heart that God raised him from the dead, you will be saved.
> (Romans 10:9, CSB)

The cry of the Apostle Thomas after encountering the risen Christ – 'My Lord and my God!' – has echoed through the centuries as one of the most profound confessions of faith. It is not merely a statement of belief; it is an act of surrender, worship and loyalty in the face of uncertainty. Thomas, once doubting, now stood firm in his confession. In our own time, this confession continues to be made, often in places where faith in Jesus Christ comes with a cost.

For the people of the CNI, this confession is not abstract. It is lived out in villages and cities, in classrooms and hospitals, and in communities where poverty, social exclusion, caste-based discrimination and even hostility to the gospel are daily realities. Yet, amid these struggles, believers continue to confess Christ as Lord – not only with their lips but through resilient lives of discipleship.

The context of the CNI

The CNI is a united and uniting Church, formed in 1970 as a visible expression of the one, holy, catholic and apostolic Church. Spread across 28 dioceses in 22 states and the Andaman and Nicobar Islands, with 2.3 million members in more than 4,600 congregations, the CNI bears witness to Christ in diverse cultural, social and economic contexts. It is served by more than 2,400 ordained ministers, women and men alike, alongside thousands of volunteers who embody the mission of the Church in daily service.

The CNI's ministry extends beyond the pulpit into 564 educational institutions, 60 hospitals and medical centres, and 7 theological colleges. Through these institutions and countless local initiatives, the Church seeks to proclaim the gospel of Jesus Christ not only in words but also through acts of healing, teaching, advocacy and empowerment – regardless of caste, creed or colour. This commitment springs from the heritage of the churches that came together to form the CNI – churches rooted in apostolic teaching, renewed by the Reformation and carrying forward the mission of Christ in India. It is in this heritage that the confession of Thomas – 'My Lord and my God' – finds living expression in the Indian context today.

'My Lord and My God': confessing Christ amid trials

Confession in the midst of opposition

The words of Romans 10:9 remind us that confessing Jesus as Lord is central to salvation. Yet in many contexts across India, such a confession is countercultural and costly. Believers, especially those from Dalit and tribal backgrounds, face rejection, social stratification and even violent opposition. To say 'Jesus is Lord' often means declaring that no other power – social, political or spiritual – has ultimate authority over their lives.

I recall the testimony of a young woman from a rural congregation in Odisha. Born into poverty and considered 'untouchable' by her village community, she found in Christ a dignity that society had denied her. When she chose to be baptised, her family was ostracized. Yet she stood firm, saying: 'Even if the world rejects me, I have found my Lord and my God.' Today, she leads a women's fellowship group, teaching others to read the Scriptures and to find hope in Christ. In another instance, a small congregation in Madhya Pradesh, despite being attacked for holding prayers, continues to gather every Sunday under a tree in the village outskirts. Their witness is simple yet powerful: they sing, pray and break bread together, declaring that Christ alone is Lord of their lives. Their perseverance reminds us that the Church is never defeated by opposition; rather, it shines brighter in adversity.

The cross and the hope of resurrection

Lent invites us to walk the way of the cross with Jesus. For many in the CNI, the cross is not a distant symbol but a daily experience. Poverty, hunger, lack of education and systemic discrimination weigh heavily. Yet, in these very contexts, the hope of resurrection gives courage.

I remember visiting a small Christian community in a tsunami-affected region of the Andaman and Nicobar Islands. Families had lost homes and crops, yet they welcomed us with songs of praise. When I asked how they could sing with such joy, one elder replied, 'We have nothing left but Christ – and Christ is enough.' That testimony still lingers with me as a reminder of what true discipleship looks like.

This is the mystery of Lent: as we participate in the sufferings of Christ, we also partake in the power of His resurrection. Confessing 'My Lord and my God' is not an escape from suffering but a declaration of victory in the midst of it.

A witness to the Communion

The voice of the CNI is but one among the many in the global Anglican Communion, yet it bears a vital witness: that the gospel of Christ continues to transform lives even in hostile environments. For our brothers and sisters in the Church of England and across the Communion, we offer this testimony not to evoke sympathy but to inspire solidarity and shared mission. To confess Christ as Lord is to join a communion of believers across cultures and nations, bound not by ease or comfort but by the cross and the empty tomb. As we journey through Lent, may the confession of Thomas become ours anew: 'My Lord and my God.'

Prayer

Gracious God, you revealed yourself to Thomas in his doubt, and he confessed you as Lord and God. Grant us the courage to confess Christ with boldness, even in the face of trials. Strengthen your Church in India, in the UK and across the world, that we may together proclaim the good news of salvation in word and deed. Through Jesus Christ, who is Lord of all. Amen.

'All you need is love' (The Beatles)

Archbishop Anne Germond serves as the eleventh bishop of the diocese of Algoma (Canada) and Metropolitan of the Ecclesiastical Province of Ontario. Prior to her consecration in February 2017, she was a parish priest for seventeen years. Born and raised in South Africa where Anne was a teacher, she and her spouse emigrated to Canada in the 1980s, quickly falling in love with Northern Ontario where they have lived ever since.

'This is my commandment, that you love one another as I have loved you' (John 15:12, NRSV)

Recently, our family bid a sad farewell to a dear friend, taken too soon by brain cancer. Fr Hamish was one of the Catholic priests in our city – a man with a deep faith, a warm heart and a generous spirit. I didn't meet Fr Hamish at an ecumenical church service or at a gathering of clergy, or because his bishop had told him he should call the new Anglican Bishop. I met Fr Hamish after one of the Symphony Orchestra's concerts in our city, as my husband Colin was anxious to introduce me to his new friend and violin partner in the second fiddles.

'All you need is love' (The Beatles)

'So,' Fr Hamish said, looking up at me, 'you're the new bishop, are you?' I waited for the stiff handshake, the dismissive wave and the promise that we would connect at some point. What greeted me was his warm smile, those piercing eyes, his immediate acceptance and the words, 'Well, we must have you over for dinner.' And that, as they say, was that. He meant every word of his invitation, and we immediately became part of his circle of friends and frequent guests at his home and dinner table, as he was at ours.

Limitations and tensions

There were limits to the table fellowship we could enjoy because we ministered in different denominations where 'full communion' and Jesus' prayer that his followers 'may be one' (John 17.21, NRSV) are not yet realised.

I cannot receive the sacrament of Holy Communion in the Catholic Church, and, while Anglicans welcome all the baptised to the eucharistic table, Fr Hamish never came forward to ours.

I'm sure that some of his colleagues found it difficult to accept me as a female cleric and bishop. Fr Hamish and I did not always agree on doctrinal and theological issues that are cause for division within our denominations. That meant difficult conversations and some tension in our friendship.

Yet, despite all the differences, I was often invited to sit at a place of honour in the sanctuary where Fr Hamish served, as he was in ours. Over the years, we embarked on numerous ecumenical endeavours, bringing our churches together whenever we were able. And as the cancer took its course,

I was invited by Fr Hamish to preach at the Vigil service the evening before his funeral, one of the greatest honours of my life.

It was Aristotle who once said that 'a friend is another self'. Friends form each other in life, taking on each other's characteristics – both the good and the bad. Fr Hamish and I enjoyed the best kind of friendship in which we both sought to emulate Christ and to cross the boundaries and the limits imposed on us by our denominations. I shall miss him very much.

Agape love for all

Inspired by Jesus' commandment to love one another as he has loved us, we are called to overcome differences, build trusting relationships, and forge new ones with people of every denomination, creed, sexual orientation and gender. It is through genuine dialogue, mutual respect and acceptance that we reflect Christ's love and transcend the boundaries that divide us. I see this spirit of love and unity taking root across the diocese of Algoma and throughout the Ecclesiastical Province of Ontario. It is far more than a warm and fuzzy feeling; it is a disciplined habit of care and concern that, like all virtues, can only be perfected over a lifetime. We have been given this holy season of Lent to practice this kind of self-giving love that is so amazing and so divine ... which demands our souls, our lives, our all.

Prayer

Good and gracious God, thank you for the gift of your love shown perfectly through Jesus Christ. Help me to live a life shaped by that love, and teach me to extend grace, mercy and

'All you need is love' (The Beatles)

compassion to others, even when it is difficult. May your Spirit empower me to love selflessly without condition or judgement. Let my heart reflect Christ's humility and sacrifice and may my actions draw others closer to you. In every relationship may love be my motive and guide. This I pray in the name of Jesus who loved with a perfect love. Amen.

Questions for reflection

1 What have been the consequences in your life of practising 'agape' love with your family, friends and neighbours?
2 How does your intimacy with God find expression in your daily life and work?
3 Have a conversation with Christ about how your life resembles his life.

Discipleship stories from the Anglican Communion

The Rt Revd Anthony Poggo is Secretary General of the Anglican Communion. Bishop Anthony was born in Kajo-Keji in what is now South Sudan and then fled to Uganda during the first Sudanese civil war, only returning at the age of 9. He has a BA in Management and Public Administration, an MA in Biblical Studies and an MBA. He worked for Scripture Union and Across before being ordained, and served as Bishop of Kajo-Keji from 2007 to 2016. From 2016 to 2022, he served as the Archbishop of Canterbury's Advisor on Anglican Communion Affairs, prior to his appointment as Secretary General.

> Therefore go and make disciples of all nations, baptising them in the name of the Father and of the Son and of the Holy Spirit, and teaching them to obey everything I have commanded you.
> (Matthew 28:19–20, NIV)

This is known as the Great Commission and was one of the last things that Jesus said to his disciples. In South Sudan we take seriously what a person says before he or she dies. So as Christians we believe we should pay serious attention to what Jesus said before he left this world. How well, then, is the

Church and especially the Anglican Communion responding to this call?

One of the joys of my role as Secretary General of the Anglican Communion is to hear and see how Anglicans at local level are living out their discipleship in many committed ways.

Earlier this year, I visited the Diocese of Mombasa in Kenya and saw how Anglicans there are putting their faith into practice by planting trees to address climate change and planting churches in villages where none has existed up to now. All this is a constant reminder of how discipleship is at the heart of mission, a key way in which God works through his people to transform the world. In the Anglican Communion we now understand the Five Marks of Mission to be especially expressed through discipleship, summed up with five 't' words – **telling** others the gospel, **teaching** new believers, **tending** those in need, **transforming** unjust structures and **treasuring** our beautiful world. Anglicans disagree on some big ethical issues of our day but we unite around the Five Marks of Mission and how these are expressed through being faithful disciples of Christ.

This perspective was brought to prominence in 2016 at the meeting of the Anglican Consultative Council (ACC) in Lusaka, Zambia. This council meets every three years and includes lay people as well as deacons, priests and bishops. At that meeting, the delegates decided it was high time to launch a 'Season of Intentional Discipleship', a decade for being intentional about growing and deepening discipleship across the churches of the Anglican Communion. There was clear resolve that deepening and strengthening such commitment is the key to church growth in the years ahead. While most

Week 5

Anglicans are happy to make promises at baptism services and recite the creeds, this does not always translate into putting their faith into practice during the week. Across the Communion, discipleship may be a mile wide but often it is only an inch deep.

The Season of Intentional Discipleship has been addressing this head on. To date, well over 100 dioceses and many of the 42 provinces have formally adopted Intentional Discipleship as a key priority and have hosted consultations and workshops on this subject. A whole range of lively and accessible resources have been produced and are available on the Anglican Communion website – go to https://www.anglicancommunion.org/mission/intentional-discipleship/intentional-discipleship-resource-hub.aspx. Their focus is on living and sharing a Jesus-shaped life. There is also a Facebook community at https://www.facebook.com/groups/anglicanwitness/about/, where members learn, share ideas, resources and good practice, and encourage a prayer network. The Season has been designed 'to encourage *every* Anglican and *every* Anglican Church to live, love and be like Jesus – in *every* part of life – for the sake of the whole creation and to the glory of God'. The vital importance of this call has been re-affirmed at subsequent ACC meetings.

But now, after the challenges of the Covid pandemic and increasing conflict across the world, we are nearing the end of the Season. Many are asking what comes next. A recently established body, the Anglican Communion Commission for Evangelism and Discipleship (ACCED), has been thinking and praying about this and has proposed something called Vision36 – a season 'for the growth of discipleship with church planting across the Anglican Communion'. At the time of writing, this matter will be tabled at ACC-19 in June 2026 I find this very exciting. It is a vision of multiplication for every disciple and every church in the Anglican Communion, in which everyone grows, and prayerfully helps someone else to grow, as wholehearted disciples of Jesus. The proposed plan is that, over the next ten years, every church will have planted one or more new congregations, or will itself have been revived. The Vision36 proposal states, 'As a sign of hope among many challenges around the world, including war, climate change and the rise of secularism, it is a vision of planting or renewing *one million* deeply rooted, spiritually healthy and fruitful congregations worldwide.'

ACCED's plan is to take three steps within an organic process: first, **planting seeds**: that is, planting the vision in provinces and dioceses, working with willing bishops, clergy and laity to build momentum and to highlight stories of good practice in their dioceses. The commission will work with theologians to uncover robust Anglican theology and ecclesiology to support the vision and practice. Of course, different provinces in different regions will require different approaches, and storytelling will be vital for building momentum.

Second, **cultivating growth**, in which ACCED will support regional learning and training where the focus will be on *training trainers* so that disciple making and church planting practices are embedded in reproducible ways. Contextual training materials for disciple making and church planting and other resources will be located, developed and signposted on websites, linked to the website of the Anglican Communion at https://www.anglicancommunion.org/.

Week 5

The third step will be **working for the harvest**, in which ACCED will encourage every disciple to help another disciple to grow; it will also encourage every church to plant another congregation – across tribal, language, generational and other boundaries where possible – with local budgets and sustainable models. It will encourage dioceses to capture their progress and share this around the world and celebrate all that God is doing.

Promoting this initiative will be an important part of my work as Secretary General in coming years and I am very pleased the Anglican Communion will be looking to the future in this positive way. It is a movement that will draw us closer together in the service of Christ's mission in God's beautiful world. But, most important of all, it will help us respond more fully and faithfully to Jesus' final words, the Great Commission.

Prayer

Lord Jesus Christ, inspire and equip us to go and make disciples of all nations. May our ministers baptise them in the name of the Father and of the Son and of the Holy Spirit. May we all play our part in teaching new disciples to obey everything that you have commanded us. Amen.

Questions for reflection

1 How might you help others in your neighbourhood or workplace to grow as a disciple of Christ? Think of some simple and practical ways in which this might happen.
2 Imagine how your own church might plant a new church or worshipping community in your neighbourhood. Is

there a shared interest or challenge that might galvanise people to come together?

Acknowledgement

I would like to acknowledge the contribution of the Anglican Communion Commission for Evangelism and Discipleship (ACCED), including Stephen Spencer, to this chapter.

WEEK 6

Listening: a Lenten devotion

The Rt Revd Riscylla Shaw serves in the Anglican diocese of Toronto, Canada. With Métis family roots, she grew up on a small farm, a child of the soil, learning from the land. Ordained a priest in 2001 and a bishop in 2017, her ministry has been inspired by Archbishop Desmond Tutu and the South African Truth and Reconciliation Commission. Riscylla is actively involved in working with the National Indigenous Anglican Church in reconciliation with the colonial Church. She is married with two young-adult children, and loves fresh air and the northern lights.

> Love doesn't just sit there, like a stone, it has to be made, like bread; remade all the time, made new.
> Ursula K. Le Guin, *The Lathe of Heaven*

In Canada, our historical Church participated in the genocide of Indigenous peoples over seven generations. In policies set by the government and implemented by the churches, we separated more than 150,000 children from their parents and grandparents, sending them far away from home to Indian Residential Schools. The goal was to 'take the Indian out of the child'. Following a Truth Commission, we are now actively engaging in justice and reconciliation. We have much work to do.

Week 6

As both the granddaughter of a Residential School survivor and a bishop in the Church, I have attended many public hearings which detailed the experiences of the survivors and their families. My grandfather would not speak to us of what had happened to him, while his sister, only once – when she was 87 years old – wept and said, 'They cut our hair, and wouldn't let us speak our language.'

This devastates me. When I hear these stories, my heart feels like a cracked teacup that's been glued back together: recognisable, but never the same.

Healing for me comes from the spiritual discipline of reconciliation. Being both Indigenous and in church leadership helps me to listen and acknowledge our Church's place in causing harm; to build bridges across Christian division by deepening relationships with those inside and outside the Church; to come alongside those who are suffering; and to learn from other intergenerational survivors. Together, we are making pathways for the future; we're living out our calling to be 'repairers of the breach', in the words of the Prophet Isaiah (58:12, NRSV).

Scripture relates the long human story of generation upon generation engaged in war with their neighbour, crying to God for release from imprisonment and oppression. As an Indigenous Christian, I can relate to the struggles of God's people in Babylon (Psalm 137:4, NRSV): 'How could we sing the LORD's song in a foreign land?'

Listening: a Lenten devotion

Keeping going through grief and despair

We love because he first loved us.
(1 John 4:19, NRSV)

Over and over again during the Truth Commission, I heard survivors say, 'I believe in Jesus, in spite of the Church.' Indigenous peoples in Canada are still struggling. Trauma, direct or vicarious, comes into our lives as a result of conflict, war, displacement, cultural deprivation and the agendas of colonisation; at times, it comes through church people or policies. Such suffering affects not only us. The wisdom of our ancestors teaches us to remember that we have responsibility for seven generations to come: the seeds we plant and the work we begin will have an effect on our children and our children's children.

Centuries after the arrival of the European settlers in Canada and the squeezing of Indigenous peoples on to 'reserve lands', some of our remote reserve communities continue to have no fresh water, and suffer from a high cost of living, minimal financial, medical and social assistance, and lack of access to education and employment. Hopelessness overwhelms some people, especially those in their late teens and early twenties. We are witnessing a plague of suicide and drug use that stems from generational trauma and continued oppression. Our future is in peril.

Yet, in some of those same places, discipleship in Christ is steadily growing. The historical Church has opportunity to redeem itself through service to the community and becoming a place of sanctuary and support.

The message of Jesus offers us real hope. He understands our loneliness, emptiness, rejection, loss of friends ... on the cross he cried out, 'My God, my God, why have you forsaken me?' (Matthew 27:46, NRSV). Our biblical ancestors wept in sadness and despair, and we ourselves grieve deeply. Living with the legacy of the colonisation and Residential School losses of life, culture, language and land, we have become a completely different people. Yet we are still here, trusting the prophetic words that God has a plan for us – that we are beloved and chosen (1 Thessalonians 1:4). Do these words resonate with you as you read this chapter?

When we are having trouble holding on to the light ourselves, we can seek help in faithful communities that have been worshipping together all these years, and in new communities forming around the good news of Jesus Christ. In the company of disciples, we find comfort and purpose because our hope is in the resurrection.

'Deja que Dios te ame' ('Allow God to love you')

Recently, while on my way to a gathering in Albuquerque, I visited a new congregation. In fact, I was feeling somewhat vulnerable, and was touched to receive the warmest of welcomes. The congregation's values of following and growing in Christ were clear to see in the way they joyfully receive newcomers and give regular learning workshops. The next day, while kindly guiding me around the community, ministry team member Deacon Judith taught me 'Deja que Dios te ame' ('Allow God to love you'). I hear this as an invitation, which gives me hope when I feel inadequate. In our human brokenness, when grief gets in the way, allow God to love you. When isolation and loneliness loom large, remember we are not alone; God is with us.

Convened in the spirit of listening to one another, the Albuquerque gathering comprised the Anglican Indigenous Network, which promotes solidarity between North American Indigenous people from Canada and the USA, South American Indigenous from Brazil, and Māori Indigenous from Aotearoa New Zealand. We share common legacy experiences of oppression and grief; of holy gifts to persist and resist. We see the effects on our relatives of ongoing oppression and new colonial practices. We are connected in struggle, connected in faith and connected in hope.

Our work of love is to make and remake relationships with one another and God, to share our hearts and our gift of trust in Christ. Whether the size of a mustard seed or a mountain, our faith is enough to put us in touch with the love and the power of God. Through generational and personal grief, God is with us.

We keep going, giving of ourselves, believing every child matters.

Prayer

Creator, we give you thanks for all you are and all you bring to us for our visit within your creation.

In Jesus, you place the Gospel in the center of this sacred circle through which all creation is related.

You show us the way to live a generous and compassionate life.

Give us your strength to live together with respect and commitment as we grow in your spirit, for you are God, now and forever, Amen.

(From Global-based Discipleship, Gathering Prayer, https://www.accnews.ca/files/A-Disciples-Prayer-Book.pdf)

Questions for reflection

1 How do we develop the courage to let God's love re-make us? Whose help do you need to do this?
2 How can we be co-creators with God of our future together, for the sake of our children's children?
3 Sit with this phrase: 'Allow God to love you.' What comes to mind? What is Jesus saying to you?

Why people in Butere follow Christ

The Rt Revd Rose Okeno was the first woman to be elected Diocesan Bishop in the Anglican Church of Kenya (ACK). She was consecrated and enthroned as the fourth bishop of the ACK diocese of Butere on 12 September 2021 at St Luke's Cathedral, Butere, Kenya. Rose and her husband, the Revd Elishamo Okeno, had four children before she was widowed at the age of 45. She has since been blessed with six grandchildren.

My consecration – which I attribute to God and take with humility – made history. Now my focus is on making lasting changes on matters affecting women in Kenya and beyond. Besides my work on the prevention of gender-based violence, I am challenging cultural practices that hold women back from taking leadership positions. My priorities include coaching and mentoring on financial innovation, single parenthood, and how to balance daily socio-economic challenges alongside the call to women to serve the Church.

The diocese of Butere is located in Kakamega county in western Kenya. It has a catchment from the two sub-counties of Butere and Khwisero and an approximate population of 315,000 people, of whom more than 38,000 are Anglicans. The diocese has 51 parishes and 170 local congregations, and we sponsor 62 Early Childhood Development Centres (ECDs), 57 primary and 34 secondary schools. My consecration and enthronement prompted the diocese to revise fully its previous strategic plan to ensure that we had a well-structured approach towards implementing our strategic objectives for the development of the diocese. The new plan was launched in December 2023. Its main focus is on envisioning 'an active and transformed Christian Community responding to the needs in society'. We are executing this through proclamation of the gospel, renewal of minds (training) and discipling. The big question for us is: what would Christ do? Paul's exhortation to the Corinthian church in 1 Corinthians 3:10 alerts us to the fact that God has called us to build carefully on the already laid foundation: Jesus Christ. How would he respond to the needs of our people? How may they experience God's love in all this?

Christianity is the predominant religion in Butere, with the ACK having a significant historical influence. In 1912, the first missionaries from the Church Mission Society (CMS) arrived. These were Walter Chadwick and his wife, who were later joined by his sister. (Butere was chosen as a second site of CMS missionary activity in western Kenya after Maseno.) The missionaries came teaching (building schools), preaching (building churches) and healing (establishing hospitals). Some of the first converts were those who donated land where the first church was built.

Many people in Butere are attracted to the Church for its ability to provide a strong sense of community and belonging, to offer spiritual guidance, and to serve as a source of hope and inspiration. In addition, many churches offer crucial emotional and charitable support, addressing concerns about cultural identity and providing practical assistance, which attracts people seeking warmth and fellowship.

However, although Christianity has had a strong influence over the years, Christian faith is not deeply rooted, and there are those who think they are Christians because of family influence – for example, their forefathers may have donated land to the Church.

Also, while people do generally follow Christ for spiritual, community and social reasons, including a sense of belonging and friendship, it is important to note that there has been a notable shift in attitude. This is particularly evident among the young, many of whom are searching for a Christianity that responds to contemporary societal needs. Their interest is in a practical faith that proclaims a God who cares about them and hears their groaning; one that translates into a deep moral commitment to building a better society; one that is strong in faith, love, justice and wisdom.

In response, our ministry is spearheaded through what we call 'family' ministries: ministries to *children, young people, men and women.* Each of these has programmes that are well designed to address specific/relevant needs, for example, those of widows, young mothers, single women and teen mums for socio-economic empowerment. The ministries also create safe spaces for fellowship and prayer.

The diocese of Butere's 2022–28 strategic plan calls for the full utilisation of the gifts and talents resident in our diocese, as well as for the establishment of relationships with our global Anglican siblings in the Communion. These mutually beneficial partnerships will glorify God and bless God's people. The diocese of Butere welcomes your prayers and fellowship in our shared mission.

Prayer

Heavenly Father, we pray that our church would grow in wisdom, knowledge and love for you. Help each of our members deepen their faith and live a life that reflects your truth. May we be filled with your Spirit and bear fruit that blesses others and honours you. Amen.

Looking at the world with new eyes

The Rt Revd Dr Graham Tomlin has spent much of his life and ministry in theological education in the Church of England. He was Bishop of Kensington from 2015 to 2022 and led the Centre for Cultural Witness, based in Lambeth Palace, from 2022 to 2025. The author or editor of more than twenty books, Graham is the editor-in-chief of SeenandUnseen.com, a website that offers Christian perspectives on issues in politics, arts and culture. He is also Chair of the Inter-Anglican Standing Commission on Unity, Faith and Order.

Early on the morning of 14 June 2017, I awoke to find a message on my phone from a radio station. It was asking for a comment on the fire.

'What fire?' I thought, feeling alarmed.

Checking online, I discovered that a serious blaze had broken out in a tower block in central London. Further quick searches revealed that the building affected was Grenfell Tower, which was located in the parish of St Clement's in the Kensington area of the diocese of London, where I was bishop at the time. I cancelled everything in the diary for the day, made my way with some difficulty towards the scene of the fire and spent much of the following days in the surrounding

Week 6

neighbourhood. Tragically, seventy-two people lost their lives, and as the horrific details of what had happened began to emerge, the world's media descended. Everyone wanted someone to interview, and the Bishop of Kensington was an obvious choice.

So it was that I found myself giving numerous interviews to journalists from TV stations, radio stations and websites. I would go into each one praying for wisdom, wondering what I might say that offered something different from the responses of other community leaders. How could I bring the grace and truth of Christ into this tragedy? As a Christian who believes in the God who turned the bleakness of the cross into the joy of the resurrection, I decided to try to sound a note of hope. This passage from 2 Thessalonians (2:16, NRSV) reminds us of the 'Lord Jesus Christ himself and God our Father, who loved us and through grace gave us eternal comfort and good hope' – even in the darkest of times.

At the end of the week, I chaired a meeting in 10 Downing Street, attended by the Prime Minister of the time, Theresa May, and survivors, local residents and volunteers. It was the first in a long series of interactions between the government and the local community. In the months that followed, I had more opportunity to try to bring a Christian theological perspective on what had happened – at a service in St Paul's Cathedral that was broadcast on national TV, and through a number of newspaper articles and lectures.

* * *

Over the next few years, I often found myself reflecting on how we, as the Church of Jesus Christ, might become better at expressing the faith, hope and love we find in him, in the noisy, often angry and polarised space of public cultural commentary and discussion.

This thinking eventually led me to found the Centre for Cultural Witness. It's an initiative that tries to harness the wisdom of theologians, clergy and lay Christians who have a calling to write and communicate the wisdom of Christ, and through the website we set up, SeenandUnseen.com, we offer articles, podcasts, video and audio material. The aim is to try to help people understand how Christian faith makes a difference to the way we comprehend the world; how it enables us to perceive the seen in the light of the 'unseen', how the wisdom of Christian faith can help us make sense of what is happening in these confusing times. Being keen to encourage younger Christian writers and presenters in particular, I've found I've learnt a fair amount myself, and I was struck recently by these words of the philosopher and neuroscientist Iain McGilchrist:

> It seems to me that we face a very grave crisis indeed and that if we are to survive, we need not just a few new measures but a complete change of heart and mind ... We need, I believe, to see the world with new eyes ... for the question is not what you look at but what you see.

If this is a world that came about not through random chance, but as the creation of a good and loving God; if this is a world in which that God has become incarnate in the person of Jesus Christ and where sin, death and the devil have been overcome through his cross and resurrection, then that surely alters our perspective on everything.

Week 6

As I continue to seek to be a disciple of Christ, I am learning to view the world with new eyes. In everything that happens – whether incidents in my personal life or wider events in culture – I try to look through the lens of Christian faith; to be open to the 'unseen' realities of the kingdom of God; to see the glory of God in the places where he is hidden, yet present. As the two blind men who met Jesus in Jericho said: 'Lord, let our eyes be opened' (Matthew 20:33, NRSV).

Prayer

Lord, help us see your glory today in the things you have made. Open our eyes to your presence in surprising places in the world around us. Amen.

Questions for reflection

1 Where do you see the presence of grace, mercy and peace in stories in the news?
2 Where do you see pain and grief caused by shutting God out?
3 How might you point others to the presence of Christ who has not given up on God's world?

The reasons why people follow Christ in our context

The Most Revd David Alvarado is Primate of the Anglican Church in Central America and Diocesan Bishop of El Salvador.

Inclusive church

The Anglican Church of El Salvador is part of the Province of the Anglican Church of Central America (IARCA). Practically speaking, the church is a small and young Christian community. It began in the 1950s and, in the 1970s, adopted a preferential option for the poor. In the 1990s, it transformed into an inclusive church, accompanying various groups in civil society and offering spaces where people from different groups can feel accepted and valued.

Young people at risk are one of the groups the church works with, offering support, training and protection. These programmes seek to provide a safe environment and resources that help young people to integrate into society. They also foster spiritual connection so that young people can develop their talents.

Week 6

Our ministry is also focused on the LGBTQ+ population. We open our hearts to people of all sexual orientations and gender identities. Our approach to the LGBTQ+ community is one of unconditional love, something similar to the love of Christ. The best testimony is from a young man, Edrian Valla Linares, who is currently a seminarian at our church and our Communications Officer for the Anglican Episcopal Church. He says,

> As part of the LGBTQ+ population, I belong to a historically vulnerable group singled out by many faith denominations. However, I decided to follow Christ in a space where I can live my faith freely, without fear of being rejected or discriminated against. I recognise that God has saved my life on more than one occasion, and that is why everything I am and have I owe solely to Jesus Christ as my only Lord and Saviour.

The church's pastor also works with people with disabilities. This is an initiative that seeks full and active inclusion for disabled people in the life of the church. It recognises the dignity and gifts of these people, many of whom suffered losses in the civil war of the 1980s in El Salvador and also due to illness.

Our goal is to make this community of people with disabilities an integral part of the church, participating fully in the liturgy and sacraments. Some of them find that the Anglican Church brings them comfort. Doña Deysi, President of the Committee for People with Disabilities, says,

> The greatest reason to join St Michael the Archangel Anglican Church is the parishioners' understanding of

people with disabilities. At St Michael the Archangel, I feel at one with the love of God, able to believe that there is a God for us. I have understood that God is with me, and my greatest task is to bring the good news to others so that they may come closer to Christ. This is my most important role, because God is good.

This is the testimony of Carlos Gilberto Reyes (age 62), who has a physical disability and is a wheelchair user:

In the Anglican Episcopal Church, I understood and internalised the fact that Jesus of Nazareth is more than a symbol of miracles performed; he is the gentleness of forgiveness and love combined, a great love that embraces our inner being. Even though externally we may be becoming weaker every day and even though obstacles – whether physical or those created by people's attitude – remind us all the time that we have limitations, in Christ I have found the peace and goodness that this world cannot give.

The Anglican Church offers us the gifts of the sacraments and brings us closer to Christ every day. People with disabilities have learned in the Anglican Church that healing is possible and that it goes beyond medical treatment, because it springs from the gentleness of love and forgiveness. The Anglican Church teaches us about a Christ full of love, beyond big miracles.

Today's young people face significant challenges, including constant change, social and political pressures, uncertainty about the future, and, in many cases, an environment of prejudice that limits their personal and spiritual growth. In such a climate, mental health has become a central aspect of young people's overall development. It's not enough simply to support them academically or professionally, we also need to provide emotional, spiritual and community support. As a church, we recognise this and firmly believe that young people need spaces where they can feel safe and heard, valued and respected.

That's why, through our churches, missions and social media, we are opening up paths of hope, building healthy, safe spaces free from prejudice. We want all young people to be able to express themselves freely, to share the way they live their faith and follow Christ, and to express their real needs. The church is not a place of judgement, but one of encounter with Christ who walks beside them, guiding them with love.

Together, we are learning to cultivate an authentic spirituality that responds to today's challenges and strengthens people's inner lives so they can continue to grow as protagonists of God's kingdom.

This is the testimony of Julia Berganza, a young woman from St Raphael the Archangel Church in Santa Ana:

> Being part of Anglicanism has been a rewarding experience in my life. I can finally get to know Christ, accepting him into my heart and life, and understanding his mission for me in the world. As one of the young people in the church of this region, I can say that God sends me out to contribute to the transformation of the world, to be part of the change, to work for God's kingdom here on earth and to care for creation, to defend and care for the human

The reasons why people follow Christ in our context

person in all its dimensions. I feel at home in the church because it builds us not only in the spirit of God, but also in the social conscience that invites me to love my neighbour.

There are many more testimonies offering reasons why people follow Christ in our context. The most important reason is because, in our context and our church, we celebrate love and dignity for the person, and we welcome and serve everyone with love in the name of our Lord Jesus Christ, especially by bringing the good news of salvation to the poor who live on the margins.

* * *

May the power of the Holy Spirit enable everyone to open their arms and hearts to love Jesus Christ through the Anglican Church throughout the world.

Discipleship stories from the Anglican Communion

The Most Revd Sean W. Rowe was elected Presiding Bishop and Primate of The Episcopal Church in June 2024 and took office on 1 November for a nine-year term. Known for his expertise in organisational learning and adaptive change, Rowe is committed to strengthening support for local ministry and mission.

As the father of a newly teenage daughter, I am reading Luke 2:41–52 with fresh eyes. In this Gospel story – the only one from Jesus' adolescence – his parents have lost track of him on the journey home from the Passover celebration in Jerusalem.

It is not the first time we have seen Mary, Joseph and Jesus on this journey. We left him here in Jerusalem on Candlemas when he was 6 weeks old, and Simeon and Anna turned Mary and Joseph's world upside down by telling them that their infant child was the saviour of all peoples and the redemption of Jerusalem.

I find it funny that the lectionary gives us this reading on the Feast of St Joseph (which occurs this year during the fourth week of Lent). After all, Joseph hardly takes home the father-of-the-year prize in this story. Here he is, travelling with a child who was greeted by angels and the heavenly host at his birth and proclaimed to be the salvation of Israel, and he doesn't notice he's missing for a whole day. Although, if I exercise some compassion, I can imagine that raising the Messiah was fairly exhausting and maybe he just needed a break.

But once they realise he's missing, Mary and Joseph are frantic. If you've ever lost track of a child in a crowd for even a moment, you can imagine their agony. After three days of searching, they find him in the Temple. For their trouble, in classic teenage fashion, Jesus gives them some lip: 'Why were you searching for me? Did you not know that I must be in my Father's house?'

Jesus, who Simeon has said is destined for the falling and rising of many, destined to upend the expected world order, starts by throwing their lives into turmoil. I am not here to fulfil your expectations, he says. I am in my Father's house.

It helps to remember at this point in the story that Luke is writing after the destruction of the Temple in AD 70, telling us a story about the old days, about a more innocent time when a boy could get lost on the way home from Passover and be found studying with the teachers, preparing for what God has called him to do.

That world no longer exists for the readers of this Gospel. The falling of many in Israel that Simeon has foretold has come about; the world is uncertain and in conflict; tyrannical imperial rule has created inequality and oppression; and many in the new Christian Church are divided one from another.

The Messiah has not returned and Jesus' promise of liberation and justice must have seemed a long way off. Luke is writing to people who have already experienced the falling.

Week 6

In this time of division and fear in the USA – and many other countries of The Episcopal Church – Luke is writing to us too. We are also experiencing the falling. The institutions and societal norms that we counted on to shape our lives and safeguard our faith have been deeply destabilised or are even at the point of collapse.

As we seek new ways for our Church to witness to Christ's love in the midst of upheaval, we can identify with the demands that Jesus is facing, even as a young boy. Over and over again in the Gospels, we see him needing to make clear that he is not here to comply with the expectations of those around him, of the ruling authorities and the established world order. He is not here to do things the way they have always been done. And just as we Christians need to change the way we relate to the powers and principalities of this world, Jesus encounters resistance.

We know that the only remedy for the anxiety, fear and division that the enemy stokes among us is to follow Jesus, who reverses everything that both we and the readers of Luke's Gospel have known. From now on, the cross comes before resurrection. Dying comes before rising. The last will be first. This young boy is not merely slipping away from his parents; he is with the teachers in his Father's house. He knows what he is about.

The conviction that Jesus is calling us to a different way, to a reversal of all we have known, is what we have to offer to our hurting world. We are told by the kings and rulers of our day that the rich shall be first; that compassion is a weakness; that allegiance to earthly power is paramount; that differences among God's children must separate us from one another;

that we should regard the migrants and strangers among us with fear and contempt.

But those divisions are not of God, and they are not of the realm God calls us to inhabit. In that realm, the meek shall inherit the earth, the merciful shall receive mercy, and the captives shall go free. There, immigrants and refugee, transgender people and the poor and marginalised are not at the edges, fearful and alone. They are at the center of the Gospel story. They are the bearers of the salvation of the world. Their struggles reveal to us the kingdom of God.

God calls our Church to make this upside-down world order real, and our vocation as Christians is to respond with courage. We must find the face of Christ in the woman at the well, the leper who comes to be healed, and the women at the empty tomb. These are the people Jesus points to as icons of the holy, and they, not the powers and principalities of this world, must show us the way.

Questions for reflection

1 When in your life have you been like Joseph, anxious and fearful about what you have lost?
2 Where in your context do you see divisions that are not of God?
3 In your community, who is at the centre of the Gospel story? Who are the icons of the holy?

Afterword: Confidence in the gospel

The Rt Revd and Rt Hon. Dame Sarah Mullally DBE is Bishop of London and, at the time of writing, Archbishop of Canterbury designate. She began her career as a nurse and, in 1999, was appointed the Government's Chief Nursing Officer for England. After training for the priesthood, Sarah was ordained in 2002 and served as a curate and parish priest in the diocese of Southwark, before becoming Canon Treasurer of Salisbury Cathedral. She was consecrated Bishop of Crediton in 2015 and was translated to London in 2017.

Not long ago, I was at a dinner of the kind bishops are often invited to attend. One of the joys of these occasions is that you're frequently seated next to individuals you don't know and get the chance to listen to other people's stories.

On this particular evening, I was beside someone new, and in the course of conversation, we ended up chatting about their faith journey. My companion had been starting to explore Christianity and, wanting to know more, asked me, 'How did you become a Christian?'

We all have our own treasured story of how we became Christians. Some will recall a specific moment, like Saul on the road to Damascus. Others might feel, like John Wesley,

Afterword: Confidence in the gospel

'strangely warmed'. Perhaps we think what happened matters only to us. But I believe that every story, no matter how simple, can offer insight into how we might bring others to faith.

* * *

I was 16 and preparing for confirmation when a friend asked me a simple, direct question: 'Have you made a personal commitment to follow Jesus?'

This was the point at which I realised that, even though I'd been to church every Sunday, had become part of that community and had gained an understanding of the Christian faith, this was the faith I'd been raised in, rather than something I had chosen for myself.

So, we prayed together, my friend and I, that Jesus would be with me. And in that moment, I made a choice, a personal commitment, to follow Christ. I remember feeling that this was not now someone else's faith; it was not just the Church's faith – it was mine.

That's how I became a Christian.

And I wonder if my friend's part in the story could offer encouragement to us all today.

* * *

I believe it's easy to feel as if we aren't the right people to invite others into a relationship with God. We might think, 'I'm not a great orator like him', or 'I'm not a great theologian like her', and that we should leave things to those who are more accomplished because surely they will do a better job.

But take a look at Jesus' disciples. Who did he choose? Not the cleverest scribes. Not the most articulate Pharisees. Rather,

Afterword: Confidence in the gospel

he chose fishermen – people who had little to no education, who almost certainly couldn't read or write, who were ordinary and no different from those around them. And perhaps that is why they were so effective in communicating the gospel to others.

When I became a Christian, my friend didn't offer me an eloquent sermon, complex theology or persuasive arguments – he didn't need to. All that was required was to ask me a simple question. And that question changed my life.

Speaking about our faith does not have to be complicated. Most of the time, it's better for it not to be. We should never feel like we aren't clever, charismatic or eloquent enough – sharing our faith can be, should be, as easy as asking a question, or telling our story.

That's because we are never acting alone. The Holy Spirit is within and beside each one of us, and always at work in others and the world. The burden of sharing the good news is not only on our shoulders. Like the first apostles, we too are empowered by the Holy Spirit, and that, for me, is a great relief!

The Holy Spirit was working through my friend that day and had long been at work within me. But one question unlatched the door, and allowed grace and faith to come flooding in. As in Holman Hunt's famous painting *The Light of the World* (one of the joys of being at St Paul's Cathedral in London regularly is getting to see this painting!), God had been knocking, waiting to be let in. Sometimes, a question is all that's needed for someone to recognise what has already been happening in their souls.

Lastly, it's important to note that the question that changed my life was not asked by just anyone – it came from someone

Afterword: Confidence in the gospel

who knew me and to whom I felt able to respond with openness and honesty.

Most often, people come to faith through their family and friends. We should never underestimate the power of talking to the people we know and love about our faith or telling them our story. The key moment in my Christian journey emerged from a simple, honest conversation between two teenagers. And that's why, at ordination ceremonies, I encourage anyone who has not encountered the love of God to speak to the ordinand they have come to support. What has brought them to this point? I know people have come to faith through hearing such stories.

For all these reasons combined, my friend's question had more power than he could ever have realised. And just as he had the confidence to ask a question, years later at that dinner I had the confidence to answer one. The Holy Spirit was at work again in the conversation with my fellow guest, who I understand is now part of a church community.

Today, I ask you to do two things. First, think about your own story, and ask what it might teach others. No matter how simple, it will have its own special insight. And second – prompted by my own experience – I encourage you to have the confidence to speak to a friend or family member about faith; to be an ambassador for Christ. It can be as straightforward as asking them what they believe, or what they know or think about Jesus. Just see where things go. You may find that the Holy Spirit has been working behind closed doors; that God has been knocking and all that's needed is for someone to push the door ajar.

* * *

Afterword: Confidence in the gospel

In my Foreword, I mentioned how rousing – but also how daunting – Christ's command could be, to 'go into all the world and proclaim the gospel to the whole creation' (Mark 16:15, NRSV). This book, with its stories from right across the Anglican Communion, has given me great encouragement. Even as it highlights our distinctness and variety, each story will have relevance for each one of us – no matter where we are as we read it. But also, knowing that we have brothers and sisters in communities across the world, proclaiming the gospel, as we are, in our shared, global ministry, makes Christ's command far less daunting. I'd even say it makes it yet more rousing.

So, as we eagerly anticipate the coming of Easter, let us head out in the confidence of our shared ministry, proclaiming the good news of Christ's resurrection. For 'you are the light of the world' (Matthew 5:14, NRSV), and the light of faith was not lit within you for it to be put under a basket. Let it shine out, and, together with our Anglican sisters and brothers, we will give light to the whole world.

Notes

'Not my will but yours be done'

1 Rowan Williams, *Being Disciples: Essentials of the Christian life* (London: SPCK, 2016), p. 2.
2 John Henry Newman, *Meditations on Christian Doctrine* (1848), www.newmanreader.org/works/meditations/meditations9.html.

GREAT BOOKS
ARE EVEN BETTER WHEN THEY'RE SHARED

Help other readers to find this one:
Post a review at your favourite online bookseller.

Post a picture on social media to share with others. Tag us and we'll share your post on our own platforms.

Send a note to a friend who would also love it or, better yet, gift them a copy!

THANK YOU FOR READING

Discover more great books at
spckpublishing.co.uk

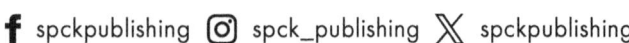

www.ingramcontent.com/pod-product-compliance
Lightning Source LLC
Chambersburg PA
CBHW070155100426
42743CB00013B/2924